Rayner Heppenstall (1911–1981) w
translator, criminal historian, playwright,
radio producer, obituarist and diarist. He is regarded by
many critics as the father of the avant-garde novel in Britain,
our equivalent of Alain Robbe-Grillet and Michel Butor.
Among his many works are several highly original novels,
including his first novel and *succès de scandale*, *The Blaze of
Noon* (1939), *Saturnine* (1943), *The Lesser Infortune* (1953),
The Connecting Door (1962), *The Woodshed* (1962), *Two
Moons* (1977) and the posthumous novel *The Pier* (1986).
The Master Eccentric (1986) is an edition of his journals kept
from 1969 to his death.

FOUR ABSENTEES

Rayner Heppenstall

CARDÍNAL

SPHERE BOOKS LTD

Published by the Penguin Group
27 Wrights Lane, London w8 5TZ, England
Viking Penguin Inc., 40 West 23rd Street, New York, New York 10010, USA
Penguin Books Australia Ltd, Ringwood, Victoria, Australia
Penguin Books Canada Ltd, 2801 John Street, Markham, Ontario, Canada L3R 1B
Penguin Books (NZ) Ltd, 182–190 Wairau Road, Auckland 10, New Zealand

Penguin Books Ltd, Registered Offices: Harmondsworth, Middlesex, England

First published by Barrie and Rockliff 1960
Published in Cardinal by Sphere Books Ltd 1988

Copyright © Margaret Heppenstall, 1960
All rights reserved

Printed and bound in Great Britain by
Richard Clay Ltd, Bungay, Suffolk

TO
R.L.E.M.R.
as stated

PREFATORY NOTE

This short book contains the author's reminiscences of four men, all dead: Eric Gill, 'George Orwell' (E. A. Blair), Dylan Thomas and J. Middleton Murry. In no case is a rounded portrait attempted or much in the way of critical judgement passed. The various encounters are simply placed in a chronological sequence which, from 1934 onward, is that of the author's own *curriculum vitae*. I should be glad to think that a pattern emerged. I will not impose one.

For the years before I knew any of my four subjects, I have turned to other sources. Most of these (Gill's and Murry's autobiographies, F. A. Lea's biography of Murry, the various autobiographical fragments Orwell and Dylan Thomas published in their lifetimes, Hollis on Orwell and so on) are available to the reader. I have touched on them briefly, all the same, and, in Orwell's case, further quoted people who knew him a few years before I did. I have also been able to clear up one or two points from the communications of his sister, Avril (now Mrs W. A. Dunn), my large debt to whom is not, however, adequately represented here. In Murry's case, I have been able to see my stare returned. I am deeply grateful to Mary Murry, who sent me typed copies of all the references to me in Murry's journals.

The other recipient of my especial gratitude is Sir Richard Rees, and to him I should like to dedicate the book. It was through him that I first met three of my four men, and we have talked about them since.

Still, in the main, I have been concerned only to set

down what I alone could personally vouch for. I could wish that all of this were edifying. It is not. I cannot help that now. Whatever I at one time thought, felt or did is of the past. Wherever it does not please him, the reader must charitably assume that I would not think, feel or do the same today. I am painfully conscious of the inadequacy of my response to each and all of the four.

R.H.

ONE

In the late autumn of 1959, I borrowed a flat in Brighton for ten days. The tenant was in America, disposing of holographs and other literary memorials, in which he deals professionally. Dylan Thomas is a speciality of his, and the flat was full of Dylan Thomas literature. In Brighton, I occupied part of my time pilgrimaging around the curious area in which Eric Gill was brought up. I looked inside the Countess of Huntingdon's chapel in North Street, at which Gill's father became 'curate' not long after Gill was born. I discovered the house in which Gill spent most of his childhood.

In Gill's autobiography, a small map accurately shows the position of this house. Gill, however, gives the address as Preston View, Dyke Road Drive. By the nomenclature of today, it should be Park View, High Croft Villas. Following an ordinary street map, I was, at the first attempt, drenched, ill-tempered and foot-sore as I crossed and recrossed the railway cuttings, looking for a non-existent house. That was on a Saturday afternoon. On the Sunday evening, a week and a day later, I returned to London. The following morning, I received in the post both a review copy of F. A. Lea's biography of Murry and the packet from Mary Murry which contained typed transcripts of her late husband's diary entries about myself. That afternoon, I coughed up an appreciable quantity of blood.

That was Monday. On Tuesday morning, I had a letter from the poet, Ruth Pitter, who knew Orwell while he was still at school. That evening, I went to see my doctor.

On Thursday morning, I was X-rayed and told that I had TB. It was decided that I should be treated at home. The alternative would have been a place called Harefields, apparently in the neighbourhood of Uxbridge. I did not recall ever hearing of such a place, but, among the books lying around my flat was a library copy of *The Letters of Eric Gill*, to which, in the hope of completing this book before I was immobilized, I at once returned, to discover that it was at Harefields that he had died.

Orwell had died of TB. So had Murry's first two wives. When I first met him, Dylan Thomas had been supposed to be tubercular. Gill had died of lung cancer (to which, one supposes, stone-carvers are prone). As I still showed disquieting symptoms, I was, after ten days on mild antibiotics, sent into hospital for a bronchoscopy, with some expectation of cancer being discovered. None was, and, indeed, after district nurses had used me as a dart-board for a fortnight, I was decided not to have TB either, though I was never offered a name for that physiological fraud which not merely coughed blood at will but simulated the right markings on radiographical plates.

Privately, I of course feel some interest in my own medical history (which, on the whole, has been uneventful). The point here is not that, however. The point is that, when I had nearly finished a book about four dead men, the circumstances of their lives and of mine could still be caught up in a web of coincidences. In works of fiction, reviewers decry any use of coincidence. I am inclined to feel that, without coincidence, there is no story. A story is simply a group of coincidences.

I suspected it before those ten days at Brighton and the rather tiresome weeks of my TB scare. The opening chapter then already drafted is, I see, full of attempts to find, in the lives of my four subjects before I knew any of them, threads binding one to another (or to me). I note, for instance, that three out of the four were (like myself)

4

brought up as nonconformists. I could generalize extensively on this fact, but as a coincidence it is slight, and it does not yield much in the way of a story, though I do think that Orwell, the only one brought up C. of E. and sent, as by family right, to a public school, exhibited, more markedly than any of the others, what is known as 'the nonconformist conscience'. The least 'provincial' of us, he also went through Dick Whittington manoeuvres of his own, first turning himself into a colonial, then going in for low life, as though he needed some remote experience out of which he could write.

After that, I seem to have tried doing sums. For instance, I note that from Gill's birth to Murry's death was a period of seventy-five years and three weeks. Gill, Murry, Orwell and Dylan Thomas were all four on earth for twenty-six years of their lives. I was twenty-nine years younger than Gill, twenty-two younger than Murray, eight younger than Orwell and three older than Dylan. Within a matter of three weeks, Eric Gill was the same age as my father. Their two mothers were, however, in labour two hundred and ten miles away from each other, as the crow flies (if a crow ever flies so far). This gets us nowhere, and yet it is inevitably true that, to me, the most important fact of all about any of these men was their coexistence with each other and with me. It is just barely possible (not, I think, probable) that I am the only man who knew all four of my subjects. The youngest of them was twenty, the oldest fifty-four, when I first met him.

All four were certainly aware of each other's existence. Murry and Orwell knew each other, though not well. Murry and Gill met a number of times towards the end of Gill's life in connection with the Peace Pledge Union, and Murry visited Gill in his last illness. I do not suppose that Gill ever met Dylan Thomas. I know that Murry didn't, though Dylan's death greatly disturbed him. Orwell and Dylan first met in my company.

My relations with all four men were closest between 1935 and '37. I had met Murry and Dylan Thomas and corresponded with Eric Gill in 1934 (and, for some years before that, had been aware of Gill). After 1936, I saw Gill only twice. From early 1937, a period of fourteen years elapsed during which I saw Murry only once and corresponded with him three times. With Orwell and Dylan Thomas, the contact was never broken for long, though it was never again so close as it had once been. So, as to period, this is a story mainly of the Thirties, though with an aftermath of seventeen years. I do not much believe in decade talk. It is produced by a trick of the English language. French literary journalists do not think much in terms of the Twenties, the Thirties (*les années vingt, les années trente*) and so on. Among those whose names are now represented as typifying the decade, I met Cecil Day Lewis towards the close of the Thirties. I talked and corresponded with Stephen Spender earlier. I once saw Auden in a theatre *foyer*. But these three did not seem to me to dominate the age. Nor, for that matter, did Orwell. So let nobody think that this aims at being a representative story. It is a personal one. I have not made it up.

TWO

Nobody talks much about Eric Gill now. His name means something to bibliophiles, typographers, wood-engravers and sculptors. Some of the London Irish may on Good Friday follow his Stations of the Cross in Westminster Cathedral. Prospero and Ariel rise over the entrance to Broadcasting House. Undergraduates at Leeds still have a relief by Gill on their left hand as they enter the new impressive portals of what are now the Old Buildings to reach what is still the Great Hall. Stonyhurst, Ampleforth and perhaps even Downside boys of the Twenties were in their formative years intellectually involved with the denunciator of bankers and the industrial world. By a strange irony, the kinds of building against which Gill revolted are now somewhat in favour. Dyke Road, from near where he lived, to the junction with North Street, where the Countess of Huntingdon's chapel was situated, is a treasure-house of Betjemanesque architectural delights.

The house in High Croft Villas is, though small, pleasantly situated, with a little verandah at the front and, from the back, spectacular views over Preston Park and up to the Downs beyond. A railway branch line goes into a tunnel under the house. The conceivable disadvantages of this are offset by the fact that at the back no further building is possible, the land descending steeply into pleasant allotments. Railways cutting through an awkward land-formation dominate the vicinity. There are sweeping curves and sudden dips in all the roads. The area is still rather under-built-up. There is no lack of trees and

7

country prospects. In Preston Park, there is a scented garden for the blind. In the main road nearby stands the Booth Museum of British Birds, an amusing folly, among whose exhibits is a stuffed great auk.

For an adventurous boy, allowed the freedom of the streets with his companions, it seems an ideal setting for childhood. The fourteenth edition of the *Encyclopaedia Britannica* shows Gill's Christian names as 'Eric Rowland'. In the autobiography, however, he tells us that he was called 'Arthur Eric Rowton' after the schoolboy hero of a novel by Dean Farrar. In letters to other Catholics after his conversion, he signs himself 'Eric Joseph', 'E.P.J.', 'Eric Peter Joseph' and 'Eric Joseph Peter' Gill. At any rate, he was the second child and first son among what were to be the thirteen children of his parents. This may partly account for the fact that he does not seem to have been an adventurous boy. Perhaps there were no boys of his own age nearby, and he seems to have been turned loose in the playground jungle of no big school. His job in the family was laying the table for meals, and his rivalry would be with his elder sister.

The long walk down Dyke Road (he sometimes resented the long uphill way back) lay past the Bird Museum, a hospital then a-building, the Dials Congregational Chapel (a Byzantine basilica, curiously ornate) and, just before the turn left into North Street, the fanciful Wykeham House. The chapel founded a hundred and fifty years earlier by Selina, Countess of Huntingdon, had been rebuilt, in Gothic style but in nice white stone, a hundred years after its foundation. It contains today an elaborate loudspeaker system, and a small extra gallery, perched up dizzily in the roof, is declared unsafe. Among people brought up middle-class C. of E. (and thus, we may imagine, by Orwell), it is supposed that nonconformists typically worship in dark, chilly and comfortless dens. Gill, on the other hand, says, 'If you've never seen it, you can't imagine the comfort of non-conformist chapels compared with Church of England or Roman Catholic ones.' When he first entered an Anglican church, he found it, 'by our comfortable standards, arid, bare and gaunt', without cushions, carpets or 'little lock-up boxes of family prayer books'. I can confirm this impression. My own Wesleyan chapel in the West Riding was warm, brilliantly lighted and gaily distempered, so that when, at the age of twelve, I first went to an Anglican service I was struck by the bare stone, the poor light and the chill. I assumed that the kneeling and standing up were designed to relieve cramped limbs by a change of posture and that the sermons were kept short for the same reason.

The Methodists proper are Lutheran. Theologically, the Countess of Huntingdon's Connection is Calvinist. It differs from other nonconformist sects in its use of the Anglican prayer book. Eric Gill therefore grew up with all that Jacobean prose which, to Murry, as no doubt to many another, was, when he first listened to it, the great attraction of Anglicanism. Gill *père* 'went over' when Eric Gill was fifteen, and the family moved to Chichester. That was in 1897. Gill's initial response was to the beauty of the cathedral and, more largely, to the order and beauty of Chichester itself, contrasted with that part of Brighton in which he had lived till then. After two years at the local art school and after becoming engaged to a church-warden's daughter, he went as an apprentice into the Church of England architect's office in London. He took lodgings in Clapham.

Murry, too, was by then actively shuttling between the southerly parts of London and West Sussex. Eric Gill was born in 1882. He was seven when the first of two sons, a darkly good-looking boy, was born, in Peckham, to John Murry and his much younger wife. London had just been made a county. There was a strike on at the docks, notoriously abetted by Cardinal Manning. Parnell was suing *The Times* for libel. John Murry was a clerk, a Unitarian, ambitious and of Welsh provenance. At about the time Eric Gill went to work, the clever young Jack Murry took a scholarship to Christ's Hospital. The Boer War took place. Edward VII was crowned and went to India for his Durbar. In June that year, 1903, a second child and first son, Eric Arthur, was born to the Blairs at Motihari in Bengal. Eric Gill, aged twenty-one, had left the architect's office and taken to earning his living by carving letters and shields on tombstones.

He took up sculpture proper in 1910. The following year, an exhibition of his work was arranged by Augustus John. That year, I was born. Two years later, on his thirty-first birthday, Gill became a Catholic. Murry had in the meantime been to Oxford, made love in Paris, taken up with Katherine Mansfield, gone into journalism and become involved with D. H. Lawrence. Orwell was not yet at Eton or Dylan Thomas conceived. I walked and was beginning to talk, though what I said cannot have been of much interest to anyone but my parents.

THREE

During the First World War, Eric Gill went into the Army for a while, but was then found jobs cushy enough. Through Bloomsbury influence, Murry went to Whitehall. The author by then of a novel, a volume of verse and a monograph on Dostoevski, he became Chief Censor in 1919 and was awarded the O.B.E. Dylan Thomas and I pursued our childhoods two hundred miles apart. Dylan's sounds rather enviable, but I'd rather have had mine than Gill's, Murry's or Orwell's. During the war, Orwell left his preparatory school, St Cyprian's, and went on a scholarship, first to Wellington, then to Eton.

There is a good account of Orwell at Eton in Christopher Hollis's book, *A Study of George Orwell*. From Hollis's account, Orwell contrived to amuse himself even in his year as a fag. The story of young E. A. Blair making a soap image of one of his seniors because he was noisy, and practising successful *envoûtement* on him, is a jewel. The trouble with Hollis is that he never seems to have stood far enough back from his school life to discover what was unique about it and what commonplace. On the one hand, he clearly thinks that only at Eton do boys touch their caps to masters. On the other hand, he expects us all to take a sympathetic interest in the sort of caning that most of us have only read about. Nobody seems to have told him that caning upon the buttocks has long been assumed by some of the male population to be a cause of homosexuality at public schools and among public school men in later life.

What strikes the outsider as particularly shocking,

however, is that much of this ritual beating is (or was) done not by the masters but by sixth-form boys. As a reward, so to speak, for sticking it out, Etonians of eighteen were allowed to spend their last year at school bruising the hind parts of younger boys. This sent them out into the world well-equipped to serve their country as colonial administrators, soldiers and magistrates, where the fags could not be expected to become sixth-form boys in their turn. Mr Hollis remembers the shiny seat of Orwell's trousers at a mass caning. Cyril Connolly, then also at Eton, states that Orwell was beaten at the age of eighteen, which to an outsider seems unlikely. Neither he nor Hollis has told us whether Orwell himself in due course became an assiduous or an expert hand with the cane.

Ruth Pitter, some years Orwell's senior, remembers meeting him at about this time, a youth of seventeen on holiday at the flat his family then had in Mall Chambers, Notting Hill Gate. She recalls 'a tall youth, with hair the colour of hay and a brown tweed suit, standing at a table by the window'. He was cleaning a sporting gun.

There was something arresting in the way he looked up. His eyes were blue and rather formidable, and an exact pair – most people's eyes are not. His sight was very keen, as I learned afterwards.

Unlike most of his friends, Orwell did not go on to Oxford or Cambridge. Unsoftened by their placidities, he went, in 1922, to Burma as a colonial policeman. Christopher Hollis dined with him twice in Rangoon during the summer of 1925. At that time, Orwell showed no sign of liberal sympathies or revolt against the imperial system. Increasingly, he later tells us, he was torn between hatred of the job and hatred of the 'evil-spirited little beasts' who made the job difficult. At any rate, there was hatred, and the worst of it was directed against the Buddhist priests. 'I often thought,' says Orwell, 'that the greatest joy in the world would be to drive a bayonet into a Buddhist priest's guts.' There was a revulsion, and in the end, 'I hated the imperialism I was serving with a bitterness that I cannot make clear.' Orwell stuck Burma for a period of five years and came home without a job.

It was then 1927. Here, the General Strike had taken place a year before. In the General Strike, 'buses and trains had been driven by middle-class young men in plus fours and others, a little older, who were in something like Orwell's position. It was the day of the ex-Army-officer vacuum-cleaner-salesman, fruit-farmer, teacher in shady private schools. At that moment, Evelyn Waugh was portraying one of them, as Captain Grimes, in *Decline and Fall*. Earlier, such men had been Auxiliaries in Ireland. Presently, they would become adherents of Sir Oswald Mosley. Orwell was of that class. At this point in his life, he was that kind of social animal. He did, for a while, teach in a private school at Hayes. But he was a man of intelligence and genuine feeling. Moreover, he had, long ago (so he tells us), decided that he was going to be a writer. Not long after his return from Burma, he wrote unexpectedly to Miss Pitter, asking her whether she remembered him and wondering if she could find him a cheap lodging, his own family having by then moved to Southwold. Miss Pitter found him a room in the house next door to one in which her employer had an arts-and-crafts workshop.

Miss Pitter stresses both how very little money Orwell had and that he was recurrently ill (with pneumonia). At the same time, he was active, and his state appears to have fallen short of actual destitution. He kept at the workshop Miss Pitter and a friend of hers had later (by 1930) in Chelsea a set of very shabby clothes, into which he would change 'prior to some excursion into the seamy side of life'. Miss Pitter and Orwell ate out together. Sometimes Orwell paid, but more often Miss Pitter. The two also met a number of times at Southwold (on the Suffolk coast) and at a week-end cottage in Essex. Orwell was trying to write. Miss Pitter and her friends did not think he had it in him.

We tried not to be discouraging, but we used to laugh till we cried at some of the bits he showed us . . . To us, at that time, he was a wrong-headed young man who had thrown away a good career, and was vain enough to think he could be an author.

Miss Pitter gives us only negative help with the problem of between just what dates Orwell lived in Paris. If, as he says of himself, he was there for as much as a year and a half, he must have been there all through 1928, but in any strict sense down-and-out rather little of that time. According to Mr Hollis's calculations (Hollis is at his most careful and excellent on all this), the 'down-and-out' part of it cannot have amounted to quite two months and was not continuous, and it cannot be said that Mr Hollis's standards of down-and-outness are particularly exacting, for elsewhere he describes the hero of an Orwell novel as 'now . . . really down-and-out' when he is reduced to an income of thirty shillings a week. From personal experience, I can vouch that on a steady thirty shillings a week a single man lived like a fighting cock in pre-war London and on an even more princely scale in Paris. By Hollis's calculations, Orwell's time in Paris was interrupted by the kind of doss-house adventures in London of which Miss Pitter was aware, and it would be in the February of 1929 that Orwell was in hospital in Paris, an experience which later gave us his study of how the poor die. The following summer, he was back with his family in Southwold. During the holidays, a Mrs Peters of Southwold, an Anglo-Indian friend of Mrs Blair's, engaged Orwell as tutor to her three boys, one of whom, Richard, then aged ten, now lectures in philosophy at Birkbeck College.

Across the estuary from Southwold lies Walberswick. For years, the two places were connected only by a ferry. There had formerly been a railway, but by 1929 this was derelict. I first visited both places in 1947. The old railway bridge had not then been recreated as a footbridge. In the late Twenties, it seems that there were only bare girders, inaccessible except to the adventurous. To cross by road, one had to go inland as far as Blythburgh. This is still the case, but in those days not so many people had motor-cars. In 1947, there were few enough cars. Despite the rusting iron tank-traps on Walberswick beach, the whole area then was pleasant. Today, at any rate all through the summer, Walberswick is a car park. On the Southwold side, there are caravan sites. Common land has been enclosed. In the late Twenties, it must all have been ex-tremely pleasant. In 1935, Orwell's sister, Avril Blair, ran a teashop in Southwold, the Copper Kettle, which in 1947 still functioned in other hands. It seems not yet to have been started in the late Twenties.

R. S. Peters remembers his first sight of Eric Blair as he came up the garden path, tall and spindly, 'with a great mop of hair waving' (I do not feel that 'waving' can ever have been quite the right word, for it was stiff hair without much kink, and, certainly, later he wore it short, parted not in but just wrongly near the middle) 'on top of a huge head, swinging along with loose, effortless strides' (well, yes, at any rate he was a quick walker) 'and a knobbly stick made of some queer Scandinavian wood'. The three boys were quickly captivated by a man of whom at first they had felt apprehensive, having heard some account of his recent history which, by 1955, one of them had come to rationalize as 'sleeping in doss-houses and acting as a bottle-washer in a Paris hotel. But he had stuck it out for a full year, and now he was writing a book about it all.' Dr Peters recalls Orwell as pre-eminently a methodical naturalist, energetic walker and practical scientist. He made, that is to say, loud bangs. He made gunpowder, and he blew up pieces of the Peters's lawn by firing it with a fuse of chlorate of potash, sugar and sulphuric acid. 'Blairy Boy for Bolshie bombs!' was the Peters's cry. Intermittently, he would take them looking for redshanks' or plovers' nests. He 'commented on the actions of politicians . . . as he commented on the behaviour of stoats or the habits of the heron' (there was a heronry at Blythburgh). He recalled teaching at Hayes and thrashing a boy whom he had caught blowing up a frog with a bicycle pump. A walk was a mixture of energy, adventure and matter of fact.

Another gifted woman writer, Stevie Smith, who knew Orwell, however, only later, once put him in a novel and made his most characteristic utterance the statement that girls were no good because they couldn't play games. Miss Pitter was spared the bangs, but about Orwell as ornithologist she is explicit.

He was very good company in the countryside. I remember so well his taking me straight to a nightjar's nest in a featureless sea of vegetation. The nest was just a little hollow in the ground, with one egg and one young bird, a very queer young bird with an enormous mouth, funny whiskers, and a valiant hiss. I expect Orwell had taken bearings on the nest, but he must have watched the old birds patiently to find it in the first place.

To Miss Pitter, being shown the nest was a nice change from squabbling about D. H. Lawrence, of whom Orwell thought more highly than she did. Miss Pitter remembers various outings.

There he is, sitting on the canal-bank, fishing, but shaking with silent laughter at something he has overheard, as two women pass behind him on the towpath. He leans in the twilight on the parapet of Chelsea Embankment, and says that the trees in Battersea Park, over the river, look very like the Burmese jungle.

Miss Pitter's eye is a poet's and vivid. I am a bit doubtful about the colour of young Blair's hair when she first saw him. People's hair does grow darker. So does hay. But Miss Pitter first saw Orwell against the light from a window, and he was wearing a brown suit.

FOUR

In the autumn of 1929, I became an undergraduate at Leeds University, reading combined English and French and travelling up daily from Huddersfield, fifteen miles away (as the crow flies). Six years before, on a commission from Sir Michael Sadler, then Vice-Chancellor, Eric Gill had finished the big relief which, placed to the left of what was then the main entrance to the university buildings, showed Christ driving the money-changers from the Temple, the money-changers in top hats, Christ (as Gill later explained to me) in a priest's alb (which showed modern boots underneath). During the early Thirties, I must have passed this relief not fewer than two thousand times. I paid it little attention. I cannot even be certain that I knew it to be the work of Eric Gill. However, Gill's features and some particulars of the costume he affected became familiar to me through photographs in the paper we took at home, *The Daily Mail*. He was shown, slung in a builder's cradle, the head bearded, pugnacious, crowned by a *béret* or a cardboard box, the hands with mallet and chisel knocking away at the figures of Prospero and Ariel which tower over the portals of Broadcasting House.

I had a friend in London, a Labour Party women's organizer with a remote Huddersfield connection. It was at her flat that I first saw a monthly called *The Adelphi*, beautifully printed, in yellow covers. Its editor was Sir Richard Rees, whom my friend had some years before nursed as a prospective candidate. *The Adelphi* had been founded by Murry, shortly after the death of his first wife, Katherine

Mansfield, during the year in which Gill was finishing his Christ and the Money-Changers panel. Its first issue had unexpectedly sold more than twenty thousands copies, but since then its sales had dwindled. Rees had appeared in Murry's life in 1927, while Murry was living in the old coastguard station on Chesil Beach in Dorset. A second wife was then dying (like Katherine, of TB), and there were two young children to look after. That September, *The Adelphi* dwindled to a quarterly. That was the year in which Orwell came back from Burma.

Here, there are the makings of a genuine coincidence. Though three years his senior and not at the time aware of his later friend's existence, Rees had been at Eton with Orwell. Orwell, of course, had not yet appeared on the scene of Murry's life. 1928 was a bad year for Murry. During its course, there appeared a volume of D. H. Lawrence's stories in no fewer than four of which, *The Border Line*, *The Last Laugh*, *Jimmy and the Desperate Woman* and *Smile*, Murry is cruelly portrayed. The same year, Aldous Huxley (a master at Eton in Orwell's time) published the most damaging portrait of all, as 'Burlap' in *Point Counter Point*. However, with the young Rees's financial backing and under his editorship (shared at first with Max Plowman, a Blake scholar and the pseudonymous author of a war book, *A Subaltern on the Somme*), *The Adelphi* again became a monthly. By the time I first saw it, at Easter, I fancy, 1932, it had also become political, Murry about that time publishing a book called *The Necessity of Communism*. This had been too much for Plowman, and Rees had taken on as assistant a raw but talented young man from Newcastle, Jack Common, an engine-driver's son.

I do not recall seeing either 'A Hanging' or 'The Spike' (part of the forthcoming *Down and Out in Paris and London*) under the name of E. A. Blair in *The Adelphi*. I do remember a poem by him which began:

> A clothed man and a naked man
> Stood by the kiphouse fire . . .

It ended with the same two lines, the clothed man having meanwhile gambled away what he stood up in to the erstwhile naked man. Jack Common recalls Orwell's first appearances at *The Adelphi* office, then in Bloomsbury Street, just before Christmas, either in 1930 or the following year. Common was disappointed to find Orwell unmistakably a public school man, who 'had not known the desperation that makes the real tramp'. He outlined his plans for Christmas. He thought he would like to spend Christmas in jail. His idea was to light a sort of bonfire in Trafalgar Square and get run in. Jack Common advised against this, having, he says, always firmly held that, if you were going to jail, you might as well have something for it. He advised Orwell to take to theft. A bonfire was undergraduate-like, and, with his background, Orwell would probably be let off. Common also remembers seeing Orwell at Max Plowman's house in the Hampstead Garden Suburb. They had met to hear Beethoven on gramophone records, but played badminton instead, Orwell much embarrassed at having to remove his jacket and reveal braces. Orwell described himself as a Tory anarchist, but admitted *The Adelphi's* socialist case on moral grounds.

In 1932, I took a very bad degree. I stayed on at Leeds for another year, taking the Diploma in Education, the idea being that I should teach. I placed a number of poems and articles with *The Adelphi* and *The New English Weekly*, whose editors I also persuaded to send me books for review. The editor of *The New English Weekly* was A. R. Orage, whose previous organ, *The New Age*, had been better known. *The New English Weekly* did not pay contributors. *The Adelphi* paid them a little.

Eric Gill occasionally wrote in *The New English Weekly*,

attacking bankers and the industrial age. As his politico-economic platform, Orage had adopted Social Credit, which I made no attempt to understand. I flirted briefly with the Communist Party in Leeds, but then settled, with *The Adelphi*, for an evolutionary materialism which was also in some way mystically tinged and which spoke of Karl Marx as a kind of religious teacher. Murry demanded 'a change of heart'. He believed in the class war, but insisted that it should be waged without hatred.

In those days, G. K. Chesterton reviewed new books over the wireless on Monday evenings. He reviewed Murry's *William Blake*. He described Murry as 'the voice of one crying in the wilderness: "There is no God, and Marx is His prophet".' I got this book from Orage. I praised Murry, speaking of his 'integrity'. Orage, clearly, did not like Murry or my review. To his honour, he printed my review, but also got a second review and printed that. In a letter to me, he denied Murry's integrity. Murry, he said, did not know what he did not know, literally did not 'sense in his own being the difference between certainty (a whole-man sensation) and belief (a mental persuasion subject to change)'. Max Plowman sent Orage a letter praising my review and taking out an extra subscription to the paper.

People with better degrees than mine had difficulty in getting teaching jobs at that time. I spent six months at home, filling up three or four application forms each week. Rees reported Murry as having greatly liked an article I had sent *The Adelphi* on Edward Carpenter. Carpenter's thought was not unlike Murry's. I told Rees (in a letter, for I had not yet met him and had not even corresponded with Murry) that I should like to do a short book on Murry. Rees put it to Murry, and Murry arranged it with his own publisher. The commissioning of this book was a great stroke of luck for a provincial youth without connections.

FIVE

In 1934, the Trafalgar Square of political rallies and pigeons was not the only one. There was also a Trafalgar Square in Chelsea. It was connected with King's Road (which crawled with young men in black shirts) by Manresa Road, in which still stand the Public Library, the Polytechnic and some very old studios called the Trafalgar Studios. It was renamed Chelsea Square a year or two later, after the west side had been pulled down and a row of small, expensive houses built there in a brown-brick, oak-doored style which makes them reminiscent of almshouses and at the same time leaves one with the uncomfortable feeling that they are not really houses at all but a block of service flats.

The numbering of those houses seems to be much the same as that of the houses they replaced. If there is a cellar at number 50, the front part of it must occupy the space once occupied by the basement room I rented from a sly, hare-lipped Scot and his splendid giantess wife between March and the end of July 1934. The upper half of number 51 was then occupied by two dear girls and a young man called Michael Sayers, whom they had acquired at the City Literary Institute and with whom their relations were blameless. Michael was a Jew from Dublin, where his father, who lived in West Hampstead and manufactured Christmas cards, had once had much to do with the theatre. It was A. R. Orage who pointed out to me that another favoured contributor and I were neighbours, for Michael Sayers did both stories and drama criticism for *The New English Weekly*.

I had at last got a job at a senior boys' elementary school in Dagenham. At first I had taken rooms in Ilford. Then I had found the Chelsea basement through the Labour Party women's organizer, whose brother, a Unitarian parson in Edinburgh, had been acquainted with the man from whom I rented it. From Chelsea, I travelled daily to Dagenham and back by District Line. There were twenty-three stops each way.

The Adelphi was edited from Rees's flat, over a newsagent's shop in Cheyne Walk, overlooking Albert Bridge. I first met Murry at Rees's in, at a guess, February 1934, while I was still at Ilford. At a first encounter, his personality did not greatly appeal to me. His voice was harsh, his laugh frequent and rather forced. From photographs, Murry had clearly been very handsome. At forty-five, he had begun to acquire a flea-bitten look, and his nose was thickened. A young woman who worked at his (and thus my) publisher's had told me that, when she met Murry, she'd always felt he was careful to display his profile to her. This did not quite seem to explain the curious way he had of hanging his head and of suddenly turning it, with eyes thrown quite out of focus, as if blind. There was often a hint of locomotor ataxia about Murry's movements. If he became at all eloquent while standing up, he would duck his head and roll his eyes, writhe and half-turn while making a point, stand up to reach his conclusion and only just recover his balance in time. I did not find him downright unamiable, but I felt that I should like to write two books on him, or one interleaved, like those translations from foreign languages which have the original text on the left-hand page. On my left-hand page I would put what I really thought. Facing it should stand what I needed to say to fulfil my contract.

At about that time, Orage passed on to me a gratifying letter from Eric Gill. I had published in *The New English Weekly* a meditation upon the fact that halfway up the tower of Strasbourg Cathedral may be seen carved the names of Voltaire and of Goethe and his companions, as well as those of countless persons of less consideration, while of the men who conceived and built the great cathedrals we know almost nothing, the conclusion being that art is best created anonymously. This was much in Gill's line, and he wanted to reprint my article as an appendix to a book of his own, the volume on *Art* in the Bodley Head 'Twentieth Century Library'. I naturally agreed. Gill was just off to Jerusalem, where he was to carve ten panels for the New Museum. He stayed with the French Dominicans and enjoyed his work.

It involved my working on the scaffold in the open sun with all the Arab workmen. I wore Arab clothes, which means dressing more splendidly than European kings and princes, and hobnobbed ... in Arab cafés and *suqs* ... We ... drank ... the wine from Latrun, by some held to be Emmaus.

That, by the way, is from Gill's *Autobiography* and not from any letter addressed to me.

I taught for seven months. I had intended to give notice after the summer holidays, so that I might get paid for those four weeks and be free just as my book on Murry came out. Unfortunately, the inspectors turned up at school while I was taking two and a half days off to revise the typescript before it went to the printers, and I was 'asked to resign' before the holidays. I went home. I did not find my position there comfortable, though, most of the time, I was able to pay a pound a week into parental funds. I had my exiguous advance on the Murry book, and *The Yorkshire Post* sent me novels to review.

At that time, I took no more than a detached intellectual interest in Catholicism. However, during those three desolate months, my current young woman, a schoolteacher, and I went to lectures on Catholic doctrine which were being given at St Patrick's in Huddersfield by two priests from a missionary house in Brondesbury. Indeed, with one of the priests, a man of great charm, the girl and I went to tea on Saturday afternoon at the end of their week's mission to darkest Huddersfield.

Eric Gill was back from Jerusalem, and a correspondence took place. It was even mooted that he and I should do a book together by alternate letters, he representing the Catholic and medievalist, I a 'revolutionary' point of view. This came to nothing, but one or two characteristic things were said. Finding my book on Murry rebarbatively intellectual, Gill averred:

The first duty of the 'artist' is to make things which people can like for the wrong reasons.

Gill's thought was, in general, of this aphoristic kind. I had read, that summer (together with Maritain's *Art and Scholasticism*, a work then fashionable), one of his books whose title had come from a slogan:

Look after truth and goodness, and beauty looks after herself.

Another slogan was:

All art is propaganda.

There was:

Art is the right making of things that require to be made.

And, taken from the writings of an impressive Indian theorist, Ananda Coomaraswamy, then deservedly still well-known, now, I imagine, regrettably forgotten, there was:

The artist is not a special kind of man, but every man is a special kind of artist.

These, it will be noticed, all have a kind of verse lilt about them. Unmistakably in prose, but demonstrating a Rabelaisian side of which I had first heard from the art master at Dagenham, Gill wrote to me in the autumn of 1934:

I wish I could get you to see the point about Xtianity – e.g. when we 'marry' we don't say to the girl: madam, you realise that what we are at is the embodiment of an idea (or do you?). We say: darling, we two persons are now one flesh – or words to that effect. It's a love affair first and last. Joining the Church is not like joing the I.L.P. or the 3rd International. It's like getting married and, speaking analogically, we are f★★★★d by Christ, and bear children to him – or we don't. The church is the whole body of Christians – the bride. Economic implications follow and are very numerous, but they *follow*. They are implications not explications.

It is, I understand, sound doctrine.

On November 1st, Gill was to lecture in Halifax to an association of high-minded professional and business men called the Round Table. Afterwards, he was to come over to Huddersfield and stay the night at my parents' small house. I had, however, by then turned again and travelled south. My book on Murry had just come out and a distinct ripple of interest was reported to me by Michael Sayers from London. I packed and went. Room was made for me among the household at 51 Trafalgar Square. By the end of the year, A. R. Orage had died, and Dylan Thomas had appeared upon the doorstep.

SIX

At the news of Orage's death, Michael Sayers and I were either summoned, or took it into our heads, to go round to the *New English Weekly* offices off Chancery Lane. The paper's assistant editor and its chief political columnist sat in a nearby pub, stricken. The political columnist was reminding the assistant editor what Orage had said in 1917 when the treaty at Brest-Litovsk was signed. His comment, presumably in *The New Age*, had been that the only thing now left of the Russian steam-roller was the man with the red flag.

Orage had been famous for his gnomic utterance. He it was, for instance, who had counselled a female musician of too great sensibility to remember that she was a pianist, not a piano. Dylan Thomas claimed that, when he first called at the *New English Weekly* offices, Orage had opened the conversation by asking Dylan whether he was a virgin. Orage had been a shambling bear of a man, with a hypnotic eye. The dislike between him and Murry no doubt had something to do with the circumstances of Katherine Mansfield's end. Though latterly he had espoused the Social Credit theories of a Major Douglas, earlier he had been involved with the fashionable mystagogues, Gurdjieff and Ouspensky. Murry's first wife had died at the Gurdjieff Institute at Fontainebleau, where the story was that she had been persuaded to sleep in the cowshed, it being a notion of Gurdjieff's that the odour of cow-dung was a specific for TB. According to Richard Rees, Orage had been rejuvenated, though whether by the Steinach operation or by Voronoff with monkey gland, I did not gather.

It was Rees who gave my address to Dylan Thomas. *The Adelphi* had printed Dylan's verse earlier than any paper except *The Sunday Referee*. Indeed, so far as I can see, it must have come neck-and-neck with *The Sunday Referee* or even beaten it by a day or two, for there was a poem in *The Adelphi* for September 1933, and I have found no bibliographical reference to any in *The Sunday Referee* before September 3rd of that year. At any rate, it was in December 1934 when I answered the doorbell one afternoon, and there he was, a chuckling cherubic twenty-year-old, with a pork-pie hat on his matted curls, a belted grey overcoat, a bit of wet cigarette on the lower of his two fat lips and, under his arm, a presentation copy of *18 Poems*.

Dylan was living in Chelsea. He shared rooms with a painter also from Swansea, somewhere off Redcliffe Gardens, I think in Edith Grove. My review of *18 Poems*, printed in the February *Adelphi*, is, I see, listed in a bibliography as the first signed review. I cannot think just when I wrote it. The next month or so went by in a haze of drunkenness. Although between two and three years older, I was less well-practised at drinking than Dylan was. In consequence, it tended to be I who produced the picturesque behaviour. This makes it less worth recalling, but I had better put down what I can. I had better put it down, at any rate, that Dylan and I together were thrown out of a night club called the Blue Mask and that, on another occasion, Dylan helped four policemen to convey me to Clerkenwell police station.

That evening had begun in Red Lion Street, where there was a bookshop much frequented by the *avant-garde*. Later in the evening, Dylan decided that I had had enough to drink and, while I was out at the back, emptied my glass. I must have resented this, for I ran my arm along the counter and swept all the glasses to the floor, after which I was myself on the floor with somebody holding my arms and Dylan sitting on my chest. Then we were out in the street. A crowd had collected, and a policeman was trying to hold me with one hand while, with the other, he fumbled for his whistle, with which to summon assistance.

At this point, so Dylan told me next day, a little man came forward from the crowd and, with twinkling eyes and the beaming face of a man about to see his life's ambition realized, said to the policeman:

'Please, can I blow your whistle?'

On the way to the police station, I broke away from my escort and got as far as the entrance to another public house, meaning to wreck that, too. Thereafter, the policemen twisted my arms. Upon my complaining of this, Dylan took hold of one arm and, with a horrid chuckle, gave it a good twist on his own account.

Eventually, I was locked in a cell. From the next cell, I could hear somebody singing to himself. This made me think I was in a madhouse. I began yelling to be let out. I called on the B.V.M. and all the saints. This was not pure affectation. Until Dylan appeared, I had been going about a good deal with Irishmen, and the characters in Michael Sayers's stories were always muttering, 'Jesus, Mary and Joseph'. The cell door presently opened, and a policeman poured a bucket of water over me. This put an end to my pious ejaculations. A few minutes later, the grille was drawn back, and a red, solemn face looked down at me.

'An intelligent man like you!' said the policeman severely, and closed the grille.

I told Dylan this next day. Yes, he said, he had just been explaining to the sergeant on duty that I was a writer of psychological text-books. Dylan had come to the police court to give me his moral support. Afterwards, we went together to the Labour Party women's organizer's flat.

It was during this period that, at Bertorelli's in Charlotte Street, dining with Richard Rees, we had met a tall, big-headed man, with pale-blue, defensively humorous eyes, a little moustache and a painfully snickering laugh. This was Eric Blair, who had published two books under the pseudonym 'George Orwell', one about Burma, where he had been with the Indian police, and one about Paris soup-kitchens and tramps. Dylan and I had gone to Bertorelli's already pretty well stoked-up on Henekey's cider. There was a good deal of nonsense that evening, too, but nothing which casts much light upon either Dylan or 'George Orwell'. About Orwell, Rees said afterwards that he saw himself as an unpopular highbrow, but was obviously doomed to success.

Another evening, just before closing time, Dylan and I were in a bar off Shaftesbury Avenue, our elbows propped on the counter to keep us from sliding to the floor.

Dylan looked sideways at me and said:

'You know, boy, if I saw you in Regent Street and didn't know who you were, I should say, "There goes a sober man."'

I brooded over this. It meant, I concluded, that, however drunk I might seem (and I had now been seeming drunk for some weeks), *essentially* I was a sober man. I was not a natural drinker. I ought not to drink. I decided that this was the truth. I would give up drinking.

As a matter of fact, I understood that Dylan himself was tubercular and had been given a matter of two or three months to live if he did not live quietly. He presently left Chelsea and was put up by Norman Cameron at his studio flat in Chiswick. The evening all that phase ended, I picked Dylan up at Cameron's, and we drank our way round Hammersmith. I cannot think what the occasion of this was, but on the embankment it seems I blacked Dylan's eye. The next I heard of him, he was in Cheshire, staying with a historian now rather well-known. He was reported to have been seriously ill.

At this point, I am tempted to type out two limericks by

Dylan that I recall from this period in his and my life, but one printer has already refused to print them even for private circulation, and the lending libraries might not care for them. They were to be the first and third of a projected sequence in which the Gospel story should be unfolded in limericks. There was also a song he'd made up called 'The Rape at the Y.M.C.A.', of which all I remember is the beginning of the refrain, twice repeating the words, 'Is this your Christian work?'

SEVEN

The Trafalgar Square household broke up. Michael Sayers and I took two rooms on a top floor in Kilburn at a combined rent of ten shillings a week. Michael was rarely there. He slept at his parents' house, where the food was provided.

I had the big room at the front. It was furnished with a desk, a camp-bed, two small bookcases, a leather-covered basketwork trunk and, generally, the wooden chair from Michael's room, which contained a proper divan and even a carpet of sorts. The desk was a present from the Labour Party women's organizer. On it stood a typewriter which belonged to her, though, as she had just bought a new one, she would never want this back. The camp-bed was hers. One of the bookcases had been sent down from Huddersfield, and the other I had knocked together myself in Chelsea. There was a fitted cupboard, and there was a skylight. There was no gas or electric light, though on the landing was a gas-stove, with a penny-in-the-slot meter. There were candles stuck with their own wax to the mantelpiece, and there were two candlesticks on the desk. I had stained the floor with permanganate of potash.

On the ground floor lived a sad-looking young woman with a helpless father. On the first floor lived the Smiths, who had two fair-haired little girls. Immediately below me lived the Stringers. The Stringers had a baby, a white cat and two boys, aged about five and eight. The lavatory was on a half-landing below the Smiths. There was a sink in a sort of cubby-hole on a landing below the Stringers. The Smith children played in the lavatory. You had to turn them out if you wanted to use it. The sink, shared by Mrs Stringer and myself, was full of tea-leaves, and the white cat lived under it.

There were always shrillness, anger and grief coming upstairs from the Stringers. Mrs Stringer spent much of her time beating the older boy. When she was out, he banged his younger brother over the head. The younger brother tortured the baby, and the baby twisted the cat's tail, had indeed, at one time, to judge by its shape, succeeded in breaking it.

On Saturday evening, between ten o'clock and eleven, the Stringers came back from the Cock, the Earl Derby, the Coopers' Arms or the Victoria, and from their premises arose screams, thumps, hoarse masculine shouts and the whimpering of children. When this had gone on a little while, I would go down to the Smiths and knock at their door.

'Do you think we ought to go up?' I had said the first time.

Smith always came up. We knocked at the Stringers' door, opened it and tacitly showed ourselves.

Stringer, panting, gave up beating his wife and said: 'All right.'

Smith and I then returned to our own rooms, Luckily the Smiths were never out on Saturday evenings.

Equally regular were my Sundays and Mondays. On Sunday morning, I went to the Labour Party organizer's flat near King's Cross. I stayed with her for lunch and tea and, in the evening, went to the Ballet Club in Notting Hill Gate. I was writing a book on dancing, and I did ballet criticism for *The New English Weekly*. This was unremunerative, except in so far as it got me free theatre tickets.

On Monday morning, as soon as the rent-collector had been (before, if the sum of ten shillings had not yet been put together), I stuffed any dirty clothes into a rucksack and went off to Hampstead Garden Suburb, where lived the second of the two older women without whose ministrations my life at this time would have been markedly less agreeable than it was. Her name was Mabel, a high-minded business man's wife. I had my bath, stuffed clean clothes and darned socks into my rucksack and stayed on through lunch until Mabel's children came home for tea (after tea, I went to the Silver Buffet in Holborn, where, on Monday evenings, *New English Weekly* contributors met.) Thus I began the week with two square meals. I also began it clean and in clean clothes.

Mabel inspired rather a fond complicity than any steady warmth of feeling. She was a woman of great energy, activated by transient enthusiasms. These, at various times, included Nature Cure, Adlerian psychology, Yoga, Roman Catholicism (she had been brought up a Catholic in Brazil), Anglo-Catholicism and *The Adelphi*. I knew her through Eric Blair ('George Orwell'). He lived on the ground floor of a house at the top of Parliament Hill Road, in a room he rented from a Jewish woman psychologist of, I fancy, Adlerian persuasion. Michael Sayers and I had dined with him there. He had cooked for us himself. He gave us very good steak, and we drank beer out of tree-pattern mugs, which he was collecting. I had also met him in restaurants. There he would order red wine, feeling the bottle and then sending it away to have the chill taken off, a proceeding by which I was greatly impressed. I had never seen it done in France, but then my French experience, like most of my English experience, had been provincial, while Eric had worked as a *plongeur* at restaurants in Paris.

Eric went to play-readings at the house of T. Sturge Moore, a white-bearded poet in a skull cap whom A. E. Housman had characterized as 'a sheep in sheep's clothing', a pleasantry later misattributed, like so many others, to Sir Winston Churchill and said to have been used by him to describe Earl Attlee. Eric had invited me to one of these play-readings, and Mabel was there. So far as I ever gathered, Eric himself had met Mabel through his present landlady. I also understood that Mabel had paid for the typing of his first book, *Down and Out in Paris and London*, and touted it round the publishers.

In Kilburn, Mrs Stringer began to conduct a campaign against me. Perhaps she thought me a spoilsport because, on Saturday evenings, I was instrumental in stopping her being beaten by her husband. At any rate, when I was out, she took to terrorizing the delightful woman who came all the way from Chelsea to clean for me once a week, telling her frightful stories of my behaviour and refusing to let her wash up at the common sink. She also complained to the house-agent about me. On the morning of June 17th, 1935, the rent-collector told me that, of course, nobody paid any attention to Mrs Stringer, who was not an ideal tenant, but that she had, if I cared to know, been saying that from my premises half-naked women ran up and down stairs all night.

Arriving in Hampstead Garden Suburb with my rucksack, I told Mabel about these little difficulties. She thereupon suggested that 'George Orwell' and I should 'join forces'. Eric, it appeared, was also anxious to move.

'There's Michael,' said I.

'Well, Michael too. I don't know him, but he sounds sweet. Let's have a party, with Michael and Eric, and then all three of you look for a flat together.'

Mabel also informed me that Eric had got a new girl. Mabel had promised to meet the two of them at the Old Vic that evening and, if possible, bring me. I did not see why not. With the light evenings, the *New English Weekly* gatherings in the Holborn Restaurant had lost some of their appeal.

It was, I fancy, the afternoon of that Monday when Mabel took me round to call on Max Plowman, who lived nearby. With Murry and Rees, he remained one of *The Adelphi*'s big three. There had been correspondence between us in the past, but we had not met. Since Murry's conversion to a mystical Marxism, *The Adelphi* had been committed to a number of extra-literary activities, chief among them the holding of an annual summer school, which this year was to be at the teachers' training-college in Caerleon. I had been invited to lecture, and a letter confirming this invitation, first received verbally from Rees, had been my last communication from Plowman.

He turned out to be a handsome, crinkly-haired, brown-faced man in, I suppose, his late forties. His face was sharply creased and his dark hair greying. Though he suffered with his stomach and took a gloomy view of the way things were going, he yet retained something of the brisk, slangy charm of the young infantry officer who, in 1917, had gone to his commanding officer and announced that he now conscientiously objected to the war and would refuse to obey any further military orders, as recounted in *A Subaltern on the Somme*. That he should do a Sassoon like this was less surprising than that he should have gone into a combatant unit in the first place, since he had been brought up a Plymouth Brother.

In the deliberations of *The Adelphi*, he represented the pacifist view, while an intellectual schoolmaster in Tooting represented the pure word of Karl Marx and Murry, with Rees in close but sometimes laughingly breathless attendance, preached the inner revolution, a change of heart. The contemporary figure Plowman most admired was Gandhi. The prophet of the past by whom he swore was the poet Blake, on whom he had published a book.

My subject at Caerleon was to be *The Natural History of the Intelligentsia*. Max Plowman warned me against whoring after the *ratio* of Locke, Newton and Rousseau, telling me that a poet should be concerned only with

Eternity on the one hand and Minute Particulars on the other, but doubted not that some inner principle of my being would preserve me in the courts of Urizen. Plowman was a man to whom one immediately warmed.

At the Old Vic, they were doing *Hamlet*. The Old Vic stars at that time were Maurice Evans and Mary Newcombe. Minor players were Alex Clunes, Alec Guinness, Cecil Trouncer and Leo Genn. I have a notion that it was not Evans who was playing Hamlet, but a newcomer, Laurence Olivier. Ophelia, I suppose, would be Vivienne Bennett.

Eric's new girl was as plain as the old one, but of a livelier and more attractive personality. Indeed, 'plain' is not quite the word. The last girl had been of a more or less average size and shape, mouse-coloured and be-spectacled, with a squint and a stoop. This one wore spectacles, too, but her eyes were round and blue, her Eton-cropped hair stiff and yellow and her person un-exceptionally formed, except that it was too broad in relation to its height, as though one saw her in the kind of distorting mirror which flattens vertically. She had a friendly laugh, and her voice was pleasant and distinctly articulated, if sometimes a bit anxious. Eric introduced her as (let us say) Jo Atterbury. Her comments on the acting and production were admirable.

EIGHT

Herbert Read's wife, Ludo, played the viola. In the summer of 1935, she played it in the orchestra at Glyndebourne, and Herbert took a house not far away, at Firle, near Lewes. The house was called Charleston (it figures largely in the annals of 'Bloomsbury'). I got a week's holiday there, and then Orwell found a flat in Kentish Town. Michael Sayers and I moved in.

I left Kilburn without regret. That top floor had become unbearably hot in the afternoon. I was oppressively aware of the sticky banister, the silverfish and wood-lice in the lavatory and under the sink, the curious smells which rose up with the screams and whimpering from below. Still, it would have been worse today. The Stringers at least made their own noise. They had no wireless set.

Moving from Chelsea to Kilburn, I had employed on my own and Michael's account a Mr Jones, who did removals with a pony cart. Mr Jones, by constant association with modest families at their moments of greatest stress, had developed a sad, unseeing eye, which looked away sympathetically from whatever necessarily engaged its companion. Dogs tried to bite him, and for this reason he wore stiff, brilliant leggings upon his lean, divergent shanks.

Mr Jones now reappeared. The new flat, too, was at the top of a house, but these were small, yellow-brick houses. Two couples lived below, both evidently childless. The ground floor husband was a tram-driver, the basement one a plumber.

We had three rooms, a kitchen and a lavatory, compactly

disposed. One of the two rooms at the front was very small, a mere boxroom. I, able to pay least rent, had this. Michael had the other front room, but seemed likely to spend little time in it. Eric had the big room at the back. In it, all eating was done, at a big, scrubbed table.

Even a camp-bed would have taken up too much of the space I had, and anyway mine was broken, so Mr Jones kept it. I borrowed a mattress from Mabel, who called the new household the Junior Republic, a denomination which none of its members thought witty enough to adopt. This mattress I rolled up during the day and spread a rug over it. My desk stood in the window.

It was a quiet, pleasant street, called Lawford Road. We were at number 50. Across the way lived two pretty sisters whose young men called for them in the evening and on Saturday afternoon with motor-bikes. We fetched our beer from the Duke of Cambridge, at the corner. In the main road were public baths. Orwell used these. I still went to Mabel's, taking one bus to the bottom of Highgate Hill and another up it and into the Garden Suburb.

In the afternoon, Orwell worked in the secondhand bookshop at the bottom of Pond Street in Hampstead. His new girl, Jo, had appeared there as a customer. In the mornings, he wrote *Keep the Aspidistra Flying*. He wore baggy grey flannel trousers and a leather-elbowed sports coat, with a khaki or dark-green shirt and pale, hairy tie. He continued to favour this style of attire in the days of his prosperity, ten years later. On the other hand, the portrait he somewhere gives of himself as the harassed author, unshaven and in a dressing-gown, is false. *I* cheerfully loafed around like that when I was working. Then I would shave and dress to go out. Orwell was astonished that I could do this. *He* felt, unshaven and in a dressing-gown, that he was unworthy to write. He was always up first in the morning and called me for breakfast. I am afraid he did most of the cooking at other times, too, if only because he was better at it. Sometimes I would bend the spaghetti into boiling water. Usually, I fetched the beer.

There was a curious lack of strength in that tall, raw-boned frame. My own physique is quite unimpressive, but it was always I who had to unscrew the difficult bottle-stoppers and jar-lids. The Indian police and possibly the O.T.C. at Eton had set Orwell up for life with something in the nature of a military bearing, but the vaulting of his shoulders betrayed a poor chest, and he was liable to bronchitis.

'George Orwell' was eight years older than I and nine or ten older than Michael Sayers. He would then be thirty-two, which seemed to me a great age. It was perhaps a little odd in itself that he should have wanted to share premises with us rather than with men more precisely of his own generation, among whom, it is true, he did not seem to have any friends, except Sir Richard Rees and, I suppose, Rees's assistant editor, Jack Common. The disparity in age will, I hope, in itself partly excuse some deficiency in my appreciation of Orwell at the time. I shall not much exaggerate if I say that both Michael and I regarded Eric as a nice old thing, a kindly eccentric. We liked him, but we did not always take him seriously. For my own part, I even tended to exploit him a little.

Our backgrounds, too, were quite different. To me, as to Michael, Southwold was little more than an outer suburb of London. Eric had been at Eton, but had received less formal education than either Michael or I. To us, indeed, he seemed ill-read. In the worst possible sense, we were both very highbrow. The kind of novel Eric wrote seemed to us not worth writing. I thought of myself as a poet, and, to Michael, prose, to be really interesting, had to be at least as experimental as James Joyce's. To us, Eric's tastes were peculiar. We did not really care for Samuel Butler, though Henry Miller was not bad, we supposed. I had assiduously read *The Magnet* until twelve years ago, and at Blackpool long ago I had been amused by the picture-postcards, but I thought it odd to make a cult of these things in adult life. It did not seem to me to matter very much whether Edgar Wallace was a Fascist or not, since I was not tempted to read his books.

I can see that I am in danger of overdoing this. Certainly, no conversations ever took place between Michael Sayers and myself in which we compared notes and decided that between Eric and ourselves there were such-and-such differences. Nor, in fact, did I at the time enunciate in my own mind a single one of the sentences above. I liked Eric. The situation suited me. There was always something to talk about. There seemed no kind of fundamental clash. I was aware of never having any money. I was aware of Eric not having much more. The difference in background would seem greater today. The provincial universities seemed more respectable then, and nobody thought Eton *chic*, for we were still in the era of the public-school, ex-Army-officer vacuum-cleaner-salesman. I did not hold his unfortunate social origins against Orwell. He lived them down pretty well, I thought.

The difference in background was in fact less than the difference in attitude towards one's background. I was not much interested in mine. Eric seemed curiously involved with his. There occurs, in *The Road to Wigan Pier*, the following passage:

A Yorkshireman in the South will always take care to let you know that he regards you as an inferior. If you ask him why, he will explain that it is only in the North that life is 'real' life, that the industrial work done in the North is the only 'real' work, that the North is inhabited by 'real' people, the South merely by *rentiers* and their parasites . . . Hence the Southerner goes north, at any rate for the first time, with the vague inferiority-complex of a civilised man venturing among savages, while the

Yorkshireman, like the Scotchman, comes to London in the spirit of a barbarian out for loot. And feelings of this kind, which are the result of traditon, are not affected by visible facts. Just as an Englishman five feet four inches high and twenty nine inches round the chest feels that as an Englishman he is the physical superior of Carnera (Carnera being a Dago), so also with the Northerner and the Southerner. I remember a weedy little Yorkshireman who would almost certainly have run away if a fox-terrier had snapped at him, telling me that in the South of England he felt 'like a wild invader'.

When I first read this, three years afterwards, a bell tinkled at the back of my mind, and I wondered whether I might not myself be the weedy little Yorkshireman. Certainly, the passage would have been written at a time when Orwell and I were not good friends. And there seemed to be some faint echo of one of those midday conversations at the big scrubbed table in Eric's room, on which there would be cheese and bread and beer. Eric may have been inveighing against Scotchmen. The few Scots nationalists then already vociferous were one of his favourite butts, along with bishops, civil servants, R.C.'s, well-to-do Bohemians, psychiatrists, Wyndham Lewis and (though he was himself at the time already a professed socialist) most socialists, including Murry.

On such an occasion, I may well have said that, like these Scots, I, on first coming to London, had felt myself a barbarian invader. If I had, it would have been to help Orwell keep going what was essentially *his* conversation. What appears quite definite in print is frequently made up of such impalpables. The distinctness of print meant a great deal to Orwell. He would praise or condemn people on the evidence of a single sentence they could be shown to have written. In this he was more literary than either Michael Sayers or myself. To us it was a curious mind, satirically attached to everything traditionally English, always full of interesting and out-of-the-way information like *Tit-bits*, but arid, colourless, devoid of poetry, derisive, yet darkly obsessed. There underlay it all some unsolved equation of love and hate, some memory of childhood nursed through Eton, through Burma, taken out and viewed secretly in Paris kitchens or upon the thresholds of doss-houses. The fondness for country parsonages, comic postcards, *The Magnet* and *The Gem*, anecdotes about Queen Victoria and bishops, all betrayed something quite inaccessible to us.

Orwell, too, had recurrent, worked-out jokes. One concerned what he claimed to be his publisher's way, in advertisements and on wrappers, of quoting bits of reviews with words missed out, so that, for instance, if a reviewer said, 'This is by no means a masterpiece,' the statement would appear on a jacket as, 'This is . . . a masterpiece.' Another of Orwell's jokes was about replying to American women readers of one's books. They always, said Eric, sent him a questionnaire, and the first question would be, 'What do you consider the most worthwhile thing in life?' To this, said Eric, he always replied, 'The love of a good woman.' Now, both these are perfectly good jokes. They would have been better if Eric himself had not laughed at them and if he had told them less often and more *à propos*. In the case of the second joke, I found myself wondering how many fan letters Eric in fact got from America and whether more than one of them had asked him what he considered the most worthwhile thing in life.

By one of his observations I was shocked. I showed him some photographs of Uday Shankar and Raden Mas Jodjana, asking him which of the photographs he thought would go best in my book of dancing. He said that he could not judge, as he found Indians physically repulsive.

So there he and I were, our daily lives very much bound up with each other, remote from each other at deeper levels. There was no overt intellectual disagreement. It was rather a matter of where the weight of emphasis would have lain. Orwell was already contemplating a guide to working-class life. With my information on this subject he was dissatisfied. He wanted leaky ceilings and ten in a room, with scrabbling on slag-heaps if possible. Himself he hankered after the simple life. He compared the process of writing, unfavourably, with that of making something *real* like a chair, on which you could then sit down. I thought him a wonderfully nice man, but confused.

NINE

On a Saturday afternoon in mid-August 1935, I travelled with Mabel to Caerleon for the *Adelphi* summer school. On the last day of the school, Murry bared his heart to the assembly. What he now felt this movement towards a purified socialism needed was a permanent nucleus of dedicated people, not, in the all-too-familiar sense, a community but a *communitas*, a place in which men and women could be educated *in* community, a socialist university or, as the word had once been understood, *universitas*. Money would be needed, but some to whom he had spoken had already offered guarantees, and it was hoped that next year the school would be held on premises of its own, that there would be Christmas, Easter and week-end schools and that, at all times, those who felt a need to renew their experience of community would be able to come and stay for a while, sharing the humble tasks and the frugal fare of those who made up the permanent nucleus, until, spiritually refreshed, they returned to fight the battles of daily life.

After the lecture, Murry invited me to come and stay at his house, the Old Rectory, Larling, in Norfolk. I went for a few days, returned to London and then went to Larling for a longer period as a kind of part-time secretary, for a pound a week and my keep, cataloguing Murry's books, doing a little other typing and helping out of doors in the afternoon. This was supposed to go on until the end of the year, but Murry's third wife and I were soon at cross-purposes.

During my first stay, Orwell drove over one afternoon,

with his sister and an old flame of his from Southwold, where he had gone for a few days' holiday. It was also at this time that, with various interested people who came in their cars, Murry and I drove round to look at empty country houses and other buildings, possible sites for the yet-unlocalized *communitas*.

One of these was a workhouse. It was too big. The last thing the caretaker showed us was a greenhouse in which grew the largest grapes any of us had seen (there were two car-loads of us). The caretaker gave each of us a bunch, and we began to eat, exclaiming on the size and juice of the grapes. The caretaker then explained that the wall against which the greenhouse stood had been the outer wall of the mortuary, so that into the soil from which the vines grew drained the slabs upon which generations of dead paupers had lain.

The late-summer food at Larling was excessively good. Murry had a cow, and we used to ladle cream into the soup. I ate peaches, nectarines and cantaloupe melons until my mouth was sore. Betty Murry had studied domestic science. She was a first-rate cook. I especially remember her lemon pies.

My feelings about Murry were already a bit complicated. He was the best-hated man of letters of his time, and it is difficult for a young and unsettled man not sometimes to admit the no-smoke-without-fire theorem to his mind. There can hardly ever have been a man so ruthlessly satirized in his lifetime. Yet, that autumn, I was most aware of my host in aspects of himself which would have surprised his foes and detractors and might have won some of them over. He kept up his Greek and Latin authors. The library I catalogued lacked nothing in English and French, old or new, and there were affectionately inscribed copies of works by Paul Valéry and others. Murry, despite their public differences, was a friend of T. S. Eliot's. He exerted himself over jobs and Civil List pensions for aging poets. An excellent cellar had been laid down in 1929, that year of years. Murry, too, was splendid out of doors. His walled garden was a wonder. Sinking new posts and straining a wire fence was enjoyable child's play to him.

True, he made a nasty gash in my right hand. The two of us were sawing up logs. Murry absent-mindedly fed me with the next branch while I was engaged in cleaning away sawdust and bark from the loudly revolving blade of a circular saw. Even then, he was prompt with the hot water, lint and carbolic acid and not at all clumsy or squeamish.

Murry's second wife, Violet le Maistre, had died three years before I met him, leaving him with two children, 'Col' and 'Weg', a boy and a girl, both dark like himself and so nearly of an age that I was never quite certain which was the elder. There was a third child, Betty's daughter. The relations between Murry and his third wife can never have been comfortable. Betty was not merely uneducated. She was also stupid, jealous and primitively aggressive. Bad-tempered, swearing and crudely derisive women attract some men. This one, certainly, was not going to die of T B. Her face was bony, her forehead low, but she was scrupulously clean, with a good complexion and finely made hands and feet. Slightly exhibitionistic, she referred to her husband as 'the old bugger' and hated his friends in exact ratio to the pleasure he took in their conversation, since in this she had no part. A man she particularly scoffed at was Max Plowman. What she considered especially ridiculous about him was that he had (so she put it) once tried to raise Violet, whose housekeeper Betty had been, from the dead. At first, Betty and I got on well. I did not mind her railing. Then she took against me too. I have in fact been tempted to believe that she once tried to poison me with an overdose of calomel.

TEN

Jo Atterbury still sometimes came in the evening. Even while I was at Larling, however, Orwell's letters had made it plain that the important person now was Eileen O'Shaughnessy, Jo rather unsuitably filling the role of *p'tite maîtresse* until such time as he and Eileen could be married.

Though in her late twenties or early thirties, Eileen O'Shaughnessy pursued some course of study at London University. I was in favour of her and had ventured to say as much to Eric. Her complexion was a bit muddy, her manner a bit forced and girlish, but she was prettier than Jo, and Eric considered her family background more suitable. Though she occasionally came to dinner, Sunday was Eileen's day. She and Eric then went for long walks in Surrey, and on Sunday mornings Eric left the house carrying a shooting-stick which he had recently bought. Eileen, presumably, also possessed a shooting-stick or borrowed one of her father's, and the two would sit propped side by side to view the scenery of the Home Counties in the manner in which I supposed that public school men were accustomed to view scenery, what time cads and bounders sat on raincoats.

I returned from Larling, with my arm in a sling, on the last day of October. I had done no more to my book on dancing. I returned, however, with a long poem, *Sebastian*, half-finished.

On my way to Mabel's the following Monday, I witnessed a comically shocking scene. I was alone at the stop in Highgate, waiting for a bus that would take me up the hill and round to the Garden Suburb. The bus came, and I approached it. The conductor held out a forbidding hand and called out to ask me if I would go to the front and tell the driver to drive straight on to the hospital. And well he might, for, standing on one leg beside him on the platform, clutching the brass rail with a left hand from which dangled her umbrella, her right foot resting on the used-ticket box, a thin woman in early middle age patted hopelessly at the point on her shin from which spouted into the air a fountain of blood. The position was curiously balletic. The conductor (who was holding this unfortunate lady's handbag) supported her as a male dancer supports the ballerina in an *adage*.

The following afternoon, when Eric had gone to his bookshop, as there was a fire in his room, I went in there and set up my typewriter (really the Labour Party organizer's typewriter) on the big, scrubbed, plain-deal table top. One bandaged finger sticking up in the air, I uncomfortably typed out my long poem as far as it went.

Sebastian begins with a desolate, infertile land and with the arrival of an expected Dionysus figure, a dancer. In the history of comparative religion, Dionysus is one of the obvious precursors of Christ. He is a redeemer and a sacrificial victim.

I was conscious of blood and wounds. There had been the woman on the platform of the bus yesterday. There was my own hand. I did not expect it to do anything but heal easily, but it bothered me for the moment. It ached in the cold, and Orwell was quite hopeless at dressing it, though Mabel had dressed it the day before and one of the young women from the Ballet Club would be able to dress it again within the next day or two. A Dionysus link with the religion of blood and wounds was the huge grapes watered with drippings from the mortuary slab at the workhouse I had visited with Murry.

At this distance in time, I cannot be sure what deep,

subliminal importance any of these things may have had for me, but they were all intermittently present to my consciousness. More to the point, however, seemed at the moment the fact that I could not see what happened next in my poem. I had got stuck with Dionysus.

There was a black hearthrug in front of the fire. I stopped typing, lay down on this and felt, through the window, the afternoon sun of late autumn upon my face. The afternoon stretched emptily before me. I decided I would become a Catholic.

It was as simple as that. Dionysus had become Christ. I would become a Catholic. The more I thought about it, the better this idea seemed. Enough of Murry's uncertain groping after a new truth. Enough of *ad hoc* solutions to the problems of society. Enough of pagan ecstasies in the face of a Nature from which, in any case, I was now once more excluded. Enough of disorder, of wondering, from day to day, what to say next about what.

Eric would not at all approve. To him, Vatican spies were everywhere. Michael would not approve, either. Michael would have to be told. No need to say anything to Eric.

The first thing, of course, was a priest. One underwent *instruction*. After that, one was *received*. The only priest I knew was the one at Brondesbury who had been giving a mission at St Patrick's in Huddersfield when I was last there. Best write to Eric Gill. Or perhaps to Wilfred Rowland Childe, a lecturer at Leeds who was both a Catholic and a poet.

I wrote to both. Gill's first communication was by post-card from Wales.

Friday, 8.11.'35

Here till Sun. morn., then I return to Pigotts. In haste to say: I got your letter of the 6th (forwarded) this morn. I will reply today but cannot catch today's post; it goes too soon. Hold tight, sit straight, all will be well. I am dumbfounded, I rejoice, I weep, I tremble.

E.G.

Followed, in the same exquisite craftsman's hand, a letter of practical advice. It directed me to one of the Hampstead Dominicans, to whom a communication would be sent. Childe also recommended the Dominicans, though he offered a Jesuit alternative in Osterley.

On one point, at least, Childe expertly laid his finger.

. . . I am very delighted to hear your news and at the same time honoured that you should make your enquiries of me. Of course I did notice in your book . . . many indications of interest in the Catholic Religion and I sincerely hope that you will find there the only lasting happiness. It is certainly a privilege to receive the gift of Faith and to return into what is the only true *Community*.

Your volume of excellent Poems is published at a happy moment!

I shall remember you in my prayers . . .

Letters from the priests themselves also began to arrive. By that time, however, I had made other arrangements.

The Reads had just had jaundice. They lived then in the Mall, behind the Dominican priory in Hampstead, in a studio flat with a Mirò, a Ben Nicholson, a Brancusi egg (or something rather like it), a grand piano and a Calder mobile. I found them different shades of paling orange, like persons returned from the tropics and still full of quinine. I told Herbert how matters stood. Ludo herself was a convert. She was sceptical about the present business. *Via* a Catholic publisher of his acquaintance, Herbert put me on to the smartest and most high-powered converting priest of them all, the Rev. Fr M. C. D'Arcy, s.j.

From Fr D'Arcy, in due course, arrived the summons:

51

. . . Mr Tom Burns tells me that you would like to see me. I am here at the above address, and if you tell me when you would like to come I will put you up.

And so, in November 1935, I went to Campion Hall, Oxford. I arrived in the late afternoon.

At dinner there was beer to drink, and, while the munching and sipping went on, a boy in the far corner read aloud from Evelyn Waugh's best seller on Edmund Campion. I had never dined in a college hall. Indeed, I had never before visited Oxford and had only once driven through Cambridge, with Murry, during the search for empty properties. I supposed that this arrangement of the tables was usual and that what I was sitting at, on Fr D'Arcy's right, would be the 'high' table. The younger men, with or without cassocks, at the other tables, were novices, postulants and foreign students of Catholic persuasion, the sons of well-to-do fathers in their own countries. A number of young Irishmen waited at table.

On the wall at the far end of the room was an outsized crucifix of some dark, polished wood. The arms were extended not horizontally but almost-vertically upward. When the reading from Evelyn Waugh had finished and conversation broke out, Fr D'Arcy explained to me that this position of the arms was a peculiarity of Jansenist crucifixes and that the one before us had come from Port Royal, where doubtless it had been subject to the scrutiny of Pascal.

After dinner, it was apparently usual to retire at once, though everybody met again in the chapel to recite Compline. Tonight, the priests and two senior novices stayed behind and drank coffee by the fire. The reason for this was that Fr D'Arcy had just published a book, *The Pain of This World and the Providence of God*. Copies of this were passed from hand to hand, and one, autographed, was presented by its author to me.

Later, everybody went into a dark chapel.

'*Noctem quietam,*' they said, '*et finem perfectum* ... *Fratres, sobrii estote, et vigilate* ... *O clemens, o pia, o dulcis virgo Maria* ...'

In the morning, I was up in time for an early mass. Reaching the chapel, I was confronted by the spectacle of Fr D'Arcy in a white garment about which a novice was winding a long white cord, while Fr D'Arcy held his arms up so that the sleeves fell away to the elbow. This sight impressed me curiously. Fr D'Arcy, I felt, was being prepared like a pugilist for the ring or a surgeon for the operating theatre. I received the impression that saying mass was an exhibition of some form of prowess and that danger might attach to it.

'*Introibo,*' said Fr D'Arcy, '*ad altare Dei* ... *Judica me, Deus* ...'

Against a setting of white linen and gold-plated vessels, his movements were as formal and engrossed as those of a classical *adage*. He himself was now stoled in white silk, gold-embroidered. He murmured like a medium in a trance or like the pupils at Legat's repeating to themselves the steps of a new *enchaînement*, while, with their hands, they made gestures and, with their bodies, half-turns as inconclusive as these.

'*Panem caelestem accepiam,*' said Fr D'Arcy, '*et nomen Domini invocabo* ...'

There was not perhaps incense, but there was a lingering smell like that of incense, and the ringing of a tiny bell. I began to feel faint. Some intolerable climax was being approached. Fr D'Arcy's movements and those of his acolyte became more intent and as if agitated. Fr D'Arcy beat his breast.

'... *Domine, non sum dignus* ...'

The kneeling bodies tightened with a harsh and breathless anticipation. I felt afraid. The blurring of my vision told me that I could not long retain consciousness if I stayed in that small, crowded room. Placing a hand upon my damp forehead, so that anybody who looked at me would at once find my withdrawal explained, I rose to my feet and went out.

At breakfast I began to excuse myself, but there was no speaking at breakfast. The young men approached their bacon and eggs in silence, with downcast eyes. After breakfast, in his small, paper-strewn room, the Master told me not to feel that I *must* go to mass yet. It might be better if I studied a missal first and was able to follow the service. He hunted under various stacks of papers on the desk, the chair-arm, the window-ledge, and produced a small and rather battered black book. He also found me a penny catechism.

Campion Hall was a new building in the Lutyens style. The woodwork was plain waxed oak and the walls distempered. In the entrance, there was a Gill plaque of St Martin dividing his cloak with a beggar, a compliment no doubt to Fr D'Arcy, whose Christian name was Martin. In the discussion-room, which was also a drawing-room, down three steps off the dining-hall, there was an old and perhaps contemporary portrait of Mary, Queen of Scots.

The second evening, a venerable Dominican from Hampstead was lecturing to a student society on the Immaculate Conception. After dinner a young priest took me to Blackfriars for this occasion.

During the days which ensued, there were visitors. Neville Coghill (later Merton Professor in succession to F. P. Wilson) was brought along to my room. The next day I lunched with him at Exeter. The celebrated Fr (later Monsignor) Ronald Knox came to dinner. I remember nothing he said, but only his big, pendulous bottom lip and the pipe he smoked. The following afternoon I was greeted at the tea-table with the news of a special, unnamed visitor. A moment later, a grey-bearded, be-spectacled, rosy-cheeked, stockily built man in his fifties, wearing a grey garment of peculiar cut, entered the dining-hall, looked about him and made, smiling, for where Fr D'Arcy and I sat. The garment he wore came down to his bare knees, below which were gartered stockings and ordinary black, laced shoes. It was Eric Gill.

I had often looked forward to this meeting. It was cordial. I was invited to go down any time and stay at Pigotts. And yet I was disappointed. This friendly, agreeable man was a little fussier, less Gargantuan and indomitable than his photographed head, his writings and his reputation had led me to expect. Perhaps it was because we met here among the bread and jam. Perhaps, too, it was not unreasonable to feel that one was being visited, here and at this moment, like an invalid in a hospital.

For the most part, when Fr D'Arcy was not at my disposal, I stayed in my small, comfortable room and read or wrote, before a hypnotically humming gas-fire. I read the two volumes of Hopkins's correspondence with Canon Dixon and Robert Bridges. I read Traherne. I read St John of the Cross. The cave and the small flame, the defloration of the soul by God, went into *Sebastian*. Christ-Dionysus became Traherne's lover-in-the-grove. The end of the poem was in sight.

Yet all this bore little relation to the ostensible purpose of my visit. I was here to believe, if I could. I was here to believe not in Christ-Dionysus, an evolving numinosity, but in the divine nature of the historical Jesus. The belief must be simple, literal. If I had come here just to finish my poem, than I had better finish it and go.

Go, perhaps, anyway. Such as it was, my own life lay in London. I had to get on with it. I said as much. It was arranged that in London I should go now and then to an older priest at Farm Street. Fr D'Arcy would be there when the university term ended. Then we could do what still remained to be done.

On the very day of my return to London, I so resolutely addressed myself to the subject of ballet that, in little more than a week, I had written a further thirty thousand words and finished *Apology for Dancing*. I had not given Orwell any address to forward letters to in Oxford, and where I had been he did not closely enquire. Our days passed as before. Orwell was up first, made breakfast, called me. We both wrote and typed all morning. We lunched together at the big, scrubbed table. Orwell went off to his bookshop. I wrote on. Michael did not appear. Jo came once, and from Orwell's room the two voices seemed to be raised in continuous argument until after midnight.

ELEVEN

Orwell was again showing signs of his winter bronchitis, but on Sunday morning he went off with his shooting-stick and a rucksack. I went to the Labour Party organizer's. There was tomato juice, bacon and salad, tinned apricots, the rashers of bacon rolled and cooked in the oven. We sat in front of a gas-fire, watching the coffee percolator.

My Labour Party friend had no strong prejudice against born Catholics, so long as their political views were not illiberal, but she saw no point whatever in being converted. Her own views were evolutionary. The evolution in which she believed was meaningful, but she saw no need to bring God into it. Man, she said, was still in his childhood. There was no good purpose to be served by deliberately reviving the religious beliefs in which he had indulged before he could walk. The beliefs, said I, might be old, but the readoption of them by myself, at this particular moment in time and with my background, contained some element of novelty, surely? No, said the organizer firmly, not so far as she could see. I was not the first convert, not even the first of her acquaintance. She deplored it all, thought it a retrograde step, leeway I should have to make up later.

That evening, when I got home from the Mercury, I was exceedingly drunk and feeling rather weak. This was not altogether my fault. I had been plied with the management's whisky. Having in my pocket the money with which I meant to pay Orwell some arrears of rent, I had bought the business manager a drink at the bar before the performance. He had invited me into his office during the second interval, and I had still been there when the performance ended.

Eventually, I reached Lawford Road. I managed to let myself in and crawled upstairs on my hands and knees. I flopped on the wooden chair by my desk and groaned.

Orwell came in, fully dressed.

'Look here . . .,' he said.

He said more than that. I looked at him stupidly, sometimes seeing him and sometimes not, hearing his thin, expostulating voice, going on and on.

'Sorry, Eric,' I said, 'if I disturbed you.'

But the voice did not stop.

'. . . Bit thick, you know . . . This time of night . . . Wake the whole street . . . I can put up with a lot . . . A bit of consideration . . . After all . . .'

Exemplary sentiments, but somehow not quite to the point.

'Eric,' I said, 'do shut up and go away.'

'. . . Time of night . . . Put up with a lot . . . Bit thick . . . The neighbours . . . I do think . . .'

I had wanted, if I could find just that little bit of strength, to roll my mattress down and lie on it. Orwell was standing in the way, nattering. The man sounded as though he might go on all night.

'Eric,' I said, 'go away. If you don't go away, I shall hit you.'

'. . . Whole street,' said Orwell. 'Really I do think . . .'

I sighed with misery, raised myself from my chair, tottered, feebly swinging a bandaged fist, towards Orwell and came to, perhaps ten minutes later, sitting on the floor in a pool of blood. This seemed to have come out of my nose, which was sore.

On hands and knees again, I crawled to the kitchen and washed my nose at the sink. I looked for a cloth to wipe the blood off the floor of my room, then decided that this was beyond my strength and that I would sleep in Michael Sayers's room.

There were no sheets on Michael's bed. I took off my jacket, shoes and trousers, pulled the blankets over me and closed my eyes. My head swam. I heard Eric come out of the back room and tip-toe along the passage. The door opened a little and closed again. A key turned.

I lay flat on my back, eyes open. This was too much. I had felt no particular resentment at being knocked out. In the state I was in, it had been unnecessary, but no doubt Eric had panicked. This locking in, however, I felt justified in resenting.

I got out of bed, and to my surprise my legs did not give way under me. I went to the door and banged on it.

'Open this door,' I called. 'Eric, open this bloody door.'

There was no sound of movement.

'Right!'

I felt strong again. I heaved my shoulder into the door. It squealed, but did not give. I kicked at the door with the flat of my foot. This hurt, but I felt one of the lower panels give. I kicked again, and it cracked. Again. My foot went through.

Then there was rapid movement. The key turned in the lock. The door opened. The light came on. There stood Orwell, armed with his shooting-stick. With this he pushed me back, poking the aluminium point into my stomach.

I pushed it aside, and sprang at him. He fetched me a dreadful crack across the legs and then raised the shooting-stick over his head. I looked at his face. Through my private mist I saw in it a curious blend of fear and sadistic exaltation. I moved sideways, caught up Michael's chair. I had it raised sufficiently to receive on it the first crash of the descending metal-fitted stick.

Then there were two other figures in the room, and Orwell had gone. The tram-driver on the floor below and the plumber on the floor below that took me downstairs. The tram-driver's wife was making tea. They put me in a chair and started fussing over me.

'We never did think much of that Mr Blair,' said the tram-driver's wife. 'Keeps us awake till three and four o'clock in the morning he does sometimes with his typing.'

'I do type myself,' I said, animated by a passion for justice.

'Yes, but not over where we sleep.'

In the morning, I went as usual to Mabel's in Hampstead Garden Suburb. I told her and her companion how, earlier in the day, Eric had called out to me while I was in the kitchen, had called me by my surname, had interviewed me like a district commissioner and, of course, had said I must go.

'Heavens!' they said. 'Keeping it up the morning after! Oh, the silly ass!'

I, too, thought it took some understanding. I supposed Eric must have been saving it up. He must be one of those people who couldn't address you directly without first whipping themselves up into a fury. I *had* got a bit behind with the rent, I admitted. And perhaps I didn't really do my share of the washing-up.

'Do you know what *I* think?' said Mabel, who at that time was interested in psychology.

'No,' said I.

'*I* think it's disappointed homosexuality.'

'Oh, go on, Mabel,' I said.

'Well,' said Mabel, 'the first time I saw him after he'd met you, he was *raving* about the way you tossed your hair back.'

I thought about this. One thing Orwell had never seemed to me to do was rave. Nor could I really see that I *had* a way of tossing my hair back. The only time we had talked about homosexuals, Eric had seemed to be

60

very much against them. I thought Mabel's theory absurd.

'Anyway,' she said, 'what do we do now?'

Orwell *could* turn me out. The flat was rented in his name.

Mabel pondered, then said:

'Jo!'

'How do you mean, "Jo"?' I said.

They told me Jo Atterbury was sweet on me.

'That might account for it,' I said.

'No,' said Mabel, 'that's over. It didn't go very well, you know. Jo told me she didn't seem able somehow, to let herself go.'

Jo had a flat in Mortimer Market, off Tottenham Court Road.

'But I don't want to live with Jo,' I said.

No need. They would persuade Jo to go back to her parents and let me use her flat. Mabel in fact arranged this there and then, ringing Jo Atterbury up at the shipping office where she worked.

'Leave it all to mother, dear boy,' she said.

So that was fixed up. Mr Jones could reappear, with pony cart, leggings and averted eye.

TWELVE

If you walk down Tottenham Court Road from the Warren Street end, the way into Mortimer Road Market is the fourth turning on the left. Mortimer Market is scheduled for demolition. The two ends of the central (as it were) aisle are blocked with sheets of corrugated iron, and grass grows in the attics. The place has been in this condition for a long time, though I do not think that it was caused by a bomb. When in that neighbourhood, I have more than once gone out of my way to see what changes had taken place. It must now be six years since the iron bracket which projected from the wall of the last premises on the left (and in 1935 and 1936 supported a sign proclaiming the name and trade of a pale, intelligent Italian-Jewish scissors-grinder, Jo Atterbury's and thus, more remotely, my landlord) was removed. Whether, like the Chelsea Trafalgar Square, Mortimer Market will be rebuilt and renamed, no doubt the contractor and the borough surveyor know. Since a warehouse opens off its left enclosing wall, perhaps it will simply remain as a yard for vans to stand in. Since a dental and a maternity-out-patients' entrance to University College Hospital have been let into the far wall, they cannot block that space up impenetrably.

Even in my time, some of the shops and some of the living quarters over them were unoccupied. A street lamp stood in the middle of the paved space between the two rows of shops. At night, the place seemed a theatrical setting for some Dickensian or Simenonesque scene of low life.

The door by which I entered (during the day it stood open) was round the far end of the left-hand row of shops. It now faces a point midway between the dental and the maternity-out-patients' entrances. Here, originally, stood a high, blind wall, the sound of whose demolition was to greet spring. The ground floor was given over to clerical work and packaging. Scissors grinding was done in the basement. Mr Fella kept a room furnished on the first floor, but lived elsewhere. Jo's flat consisted of one room and a kitchen, with a scullery. The lavatory was in the basement, near the machinery, which shrieked during the day and sweated quietly at night.

The walls of both rooms were distempered a pale green. The woodwork also was pale-green. There was dark-green linoleum on the floor. The flat had its own containing door, with a top panel of knobbly glass. This door had been set squarely at the head of the narrow staircase and opened outward, so that letting oneself into the flat involved first releasing the door and then stepping backward down two or three steps and edging round it, remembering also to pull it to again before it had swung too far back against the wall.

The kitchen had a fitted dresser and a small table of (pale-green) painted deal. Jo's crockery was pale-green and designed according to principles which Herbert Read might have passed with some misgiving. In the other room, there was a gas-fire and on either side of it a fitted cupboard. There was also a divan bed, a small plain-oak bookcase, a wastepaper box of plywood painted a bright red and a tiny, cretonne-covered armchair intended either for a child or for a dog. To these were now added my own few sticks. A crucifix hung from a drawing-pin on the wall.

Jo Atterbury's parents lived in Hampstead, near Eric's bookshop. The shipping office Jo worked in lay some-where in the neighbourhood of Russell Square. Jo also did literary typing and hoped one day to set up a typing bureau or even a literary agency of her own. With, at first, some frequency, she would call at the flat on her way from work, dust the furniture, make the bed and continue on her way home to her parents'. Sometimes, when she knew that I should be out, she spent an evening or a Sunday in the flat, typing. As time went on, she appeared less frequently.

The whole position was, I supposed, an odd one. This young woman, whom I did not dislike, now in effect paid my rent, as well as supplying me with a fortnightly change of bed-linen and even, from time to time, bringing in food. She was said by Mabel to be in love with me. It seemed possible, since she had given up, for my benefit, all the independent life she had made for herself. It was touching, embarrassing, convenient, not easily explained to an outsider and possibly best not thought about, if, as appeared to be the case, I was to be allowed not to think about it. The stirrings of conscience were faint. If Jo liked it that way, there seemed no reason why I should entertain guilty and uncomfortable reflections.

I had plenty to occupy my mind, none of it particularly comfortable. I was in rather a muddle with a girl, a dancer. The lack of money was sometimes a bit oppressive. And I was finding it difficult to give full and literal credence to what Catholics are supposed to believe. At the same time, I had found a Catholic world I liked among the group of young people centred upon a quarterly magazine called *Colosseum*. It was edited, between Seven Dials and the Strand, in a large, shabby flat, the home of Bernard and Barbara Wall, who had not long been married. I was first taken to see them by Fr D'Arcy's publisher friend.

Colosseum offered its readers a 'true' or 'integral' humanism, which involved the recognition of man's dual nature. It was against Capitalism, which it considered an essentially nineteenth-century, Protestant phenomenon, but declared that Communism was merely Capitalism in its ultimate phase. 'UTOPIAS', insisted a strip of paper folded over the cover of the magazine, 'ARE THE OPIUM OF THE PEOPLE'. The one modern non-Catholic writer of whom it approved was D. H. Lawrence, and Lawrence's mistakes it knew how to correct. It attacked Murry (I did not mind this). The plights of Aldous Huxley and John Cowper Powys it viewed with sympathy. There was, however, it said, more depth in the art of Greta Garbo, Marlene Dietrich and René Clair than in all but a handful of contemporary writers.

Some of these notions appealed to me. At others I looked askance. I was prepared to accept and even to welcome a total revision of my own attitudes. Yet it was still the case that I approached Catholicism from the Left. I remained suspicious of attitudes which struck me as Fascist, as did editorial notes on, for instance, the assassination of Dolfuss or a Swiss Catholic's view of Italy from her northern frontier, judiciously admiring Mussolini's foreign policy. On politics, I preferred the writings of Eric Gill, who, though, like Orage, he had espoused Major Douglas's economic theories, yet genuinely hated injustice and privilege and felt deeply for the humble victims of the industrialist and the financier. Gill himself wrote in *Colosseum*, though infrequently.

On all sides, there was movement. I saw less of Michael Sayers, who, indeed, presently left for New York, where he was to be Norman Bel Geddes's English play-editor. The Walls themselves went to Switzerland. In January, I had a letter from Dylan Thomas, dated the 31st of December. It reached me covered with multiple re-addressings, one of them in Orwell's hand.

Dylan was at his parents' house in Swansea. He had spent the previous summer in Donegal and done, he said, a lot of good work there. He was now 'taking a rest at home away from the beards and bow ties', though 'a wave of rather alcoholic laziness' had set in. He expected to come to London early in February. We were then to meet 'and, over beer, roar our poems at each other like little Bellocs'. On the other hand, we were also to take a flat together in Limehouse 'and write books like Thomas Burke'. A mutual acquaintance had informed Dylan by post that I was now 'utterly tamed and pugnacious no longer'. Dylan implored me to be pugnacious once more, 'just once more, and attack . . . like a bloodhound' another mutual acquaintance who had written an insulting review of my *First Poems*.

Shortly after the receipt of this letter, the young publishing lady who had described Murry as always turning his profile to her asked me if I was reviewing books for *The South Wales Echo*. When I said that I wasn't, she told me that Dylan Thomas had written to the firm for which she worked soliciting review copies of their books and giving my name and that of the mutual acquaintance who had said I was no longer pugnacious as two of his reviewers. I at once wrote to Dylan to report this unfortunate exchange. At the bottom of his reply, he did a little drawing of himself, with a balloon coming out of his mouth, in which was printed, 'Please, Messrs Cape, don't lock me up!'

Dylan appeared in Mortimer Market on Wednesday, the 12th of February, in the morning. He wanted, his last note had said, 'a nice, clean pub, with no beards in it', but we set off towards Charlotte Street, which then abounded in beards. As we went out into the cold, Dylan began to cough and spit.

He looked down at his spittle in the roadway and said: 'Blood, boy! That's the stuff!'

We drank first at the Fitzroy, then I fancy at the Northumberland (which Dylan liked because of the Bushmills whisky), then certainly at the Wheatsheaf. By three o'clock, we had picked up a party which adjourned for the afternoon to a flat off Holborn, with beer in flagons. At half past five, Dylan and I went out again. We were now on the beat of the famous evening which had ended with me in a police cell in Clerkenwell.

Dylan was uncertain where he was going to stay the night. There was my floor. There were possible beds elsewhere. There was one in a Bloomsbury square. A telephone call was made from a kiosk, and Dylan decided on a bed.

As we rolled along Euston Road, he suddenly raised miserable eyes and said:

'O God, I'm so tired of sleeping with women I don't even like!'

I, too, was in a morbid state. For one thing, I was strictly penniless. That evening with Dylan had no immediate sequel, because it had cleaned me out. Lighting the gas-fire on my return to Mortimer Market, I was depressed to see that, almost immediately, the jets began to plop out one by one, while I was without a shilling to revive them. For too long thereafter, I lived on a bag of flour and a packet of lard, left among Jo Atterbury's stores. Orwell had taught me to make, as a trimming at breakfast, what he called 'gravy dips'. These were spoonfuls of flour paste dropped into the hot fat in a frying pan. They were very nice, but now they formed too important a part of my diet.

THIRTEEN

I can see that too much of my own life is getting into this. It does seem, however, necessary further to explain that in late February or early March, 1936, I foolishly travelled abroad with the advance I had on *Apology for Dancing* and that in due course I found myself stranded in Brussels. My state of mind was, to say the least, unsettled. In this state of mind, immediately upon my return to England, I went to stay with Eric Gill. It was not yet Easter.

Five shillingsworth of taxi took me out of High Wycombe, along some miles of country road and up a steep hill, with fields on one side (the left) and woods on the other. As the gradient flattened and a wisp of smoke showed above the trees, I paid off the taxi, ashamed to be seen arriving in so extravagant and so modern a conveyance.

It must have been that wisp of smoke, though it did not hover and descend, which produced the incense-like smell. Woodsmoke I should discover to be the ambience of Pigotts. Disappointingly, the squirrels in the trees were grey.

There seemed to be almost a hamlet. There were long, tarred sheds, one of great height, and there were two cottages beside Gill's house. This was the last thing one came to. As I passed through the wicket gate, there was first a cottage.

Tea was in the studio, at the back, beyond it the high shed. There were bedrooms above the studio. Mrs Gill, a small, frail woman with spectacles atilt upon her nose, had briefly appeared and presently withdrawn. A girl

68

brought in a tray. She, too, was small and wore spectacles. She was a happy smiler.

The next member of the community I met was Gordian, Gill's adopted son, a silent, heavily built youth, on fire with pimples. Two Gill daughters lived with their husbands in the two cottages. They were Joan and Petra. Their husbands were René Hague and Denis Tegetmeier. Hague seemed to be in charge of the printing. Tegetmeier was a cartoonist. Hague and Joan were coming to dinner. Tegetmeier and Petra would look in afterwards.

There was also Father Bernard. Father Bernard had come from some monastery in the north, by way of a nervous breakdown and a sort of Catholic psychoanalyst. It was convenient for Gill, because it gave him a chaplain. Father Bernard was an authority on plainsong.

In the shed beyond the studio, an outsize Virgin and Child stood roughed out in stone. It had the familiar long, straight Gill lines, the naïve and tender gesticulation of hands and repose of feet, the medieval innocence of feature, the stylized folds of drapery, the suggestion of mere relief in what was nevertheless fully dimensioned sculpture.

'Man's proudest adornment,' said Gill, and touched part of the standing Christ-child above the Virgin's elongated hand on his thigh. 'After all, since in his physical nature he was every inch a man, Jesus must have had proper genitals.'

Reminded that he too was a man, my host led me out by a side door of the shed, to make water, as he said, in the broad light of day and to the greater glory of God. To perform this operation, Gill, wearing the short grey habit he judged appropriate to his membership of the Third Order of St Dominic, had no fly-buttons to deal with. Women, he considered, were unlucky. They had to squat down. At Ditchling, however, one old woman was said to be able to pee over the church wall. Gill had never seen her perform this feat, but had asked a local tradesman how she did it.

'Oh,' the tradesman had said, 'she has a trick of pinching herself like this.'

And my host demonstrated.

We returned through the studio proper, which was also the library and where the apparatus for wood-engraving was laid out on a large, low table. It was dusk when we came to the chapel. This looked new. Everything was very plain and white. The only statue and the crucifix were already covered with pieces of purple cloth, it being the Saturday before Passion Sunday. The girl was standing on tip-toe, trimming, then lighting, the lamp. This would burn all night, a bubble of flame adrift upon a little sea of oil, which, as the glass was pink, itself appeared rosily flushed.

We returned to the studio and were brought a jug of ale and three pewter tankards. Just before dinner, René Hague joined us, Joan having stayed in the dining-room with her mother. Hague was a tall, handsome, pale young man, with spectacles and wild black hair. He spoke rapidly and with vehemence.

At dinner, his vehemence was principally directed against Father Bernard, a white-haired but not at all aged priest, whose air was one of great benignity. René Hague's views were strongly anti-clerical. Indeed, he seemed to be rather against religion altogether. There was some talk of birth-control, a subject with which I had found young Catholics to be generally obsessed.

Joan was a small, fair, intelligent, attractive young woman, but she too wore spectacles. That made six people with spectacles, both the senior Gills, Father Bernard, Hague, Joan and the busy girl who now waited at table. The weakness of their eyesight was perhaps due to lamp-light and wood smoke. Father Bernard said grace. Gordian, who did not wear spectacles, read aloud from what I suppose was Butler's *Lives of the Saints*.

Tegetmeier and Petra came in as the girl was serving coffee. Neither of these two wore spectacles. Nobody seemed much worried by Hague's vehemence. Every now and then, as it betrayed him into blasphemy or coarseness, he would stop and apologize.

'Sorry, Bernard,' he would snarl. 'Cloth and all that.'

The Tegetmeiers did not stay long. As each of his daughters left him, Gill made a sign of the cross on her forehead with his thumb.

It was Saturday. Next morning, Father Bernard pulled twenty or thirty times at the rope which rang a bell set under the frosty eaves, then went inside to vest himself. Gordian was server. In addition to the household, there were two families from the neighbourhood in the chapel. The young man with a beard, who wore a habit rather like his master's, was a pupil of Gill's. The Hagues and the Tegetmeiers must have gone elsewhere to church.

Splendidly coped and stoled in purple, Father Bernard murmured his faint, deprecating Latin, reminding us all of the way of the cross to be trod soon. Among the bowed heads and the boot-soles, I felt no suffocation, even when the sacring bell rang and the magic began. The liturgical pattern, I thought, was very beautiful. Whatever the weather, spring in the church was always punctual. Whether hazel and willow had put out their catkins or not, it would be Palm Sunday a week today. Even without belief, there should be ritual.

It was also a nice thought that the state of Father Bernard's nerves did not render him less effective in his priestly function. The magic would happen for him just as well as for anybody else. When it did, he would look surprised and gratified.

The week went by. In the mornings, I generally stayed in the studio, cataloguing the books and sticking in *Ex Libris*. Overhead, there would sound a curious wailing from Father Bernard's room.

When I first heard this sharp cry break out on Monday morning, I had supposed that Father Bernard was either having a fit or whipping himself. Gill, however, had quickly reassured me. It appeared that Father Bernard's vocal cords were not all they might be and that he was studying a new method of voice-production, invented by a man called White, in which the vocal cords were dispensed with altogether and the notes produced by expansion and contraction of the sinuses. This did not seem to me possible.

Gill was currently engaged on a set of illustrations to some fine book for collectors. It was not of a religious nature, but dealt with a drowned sailor and an underwater maiden, who was not quite a mermaid, since she had no tail. Two consecutive illustrations, meant to lie at the foot of the page, showed, here, the sailor and, there, the maiden, swimming through curly waves. Gill sat palming his graver between the edges of the boxwood grain and then inking the block and drawing off a print. He worked with a jeweller's magnifying glass in his eye.

'There,' he said, 'they'll do.'

He patted and stroked the air over the damp and glistening block which showed the underwater lady.

'Dear little bottom she's got, don't you think?'

I went across to look. Yes, she had a nice little bottom. And I went on cataloguing the books and sticking in *Ex Libris*. In one of the books, I came across a set of wood-engravings which, if they had been photographs, would have been thought (and would have been) obscene. They showed a pair of lovers in various postures of ecstasy, not, perhaps, illustrating all the recognized 'positions', but versatile for all that and curiously beautiful.

On Thursday, there came a letter from Fr D'Arcy, 'relieved' to hear I was back again.

And where better than at Pigotts? I think such a serenity has its home there.

I was to keep in touch. Like death and truth, Catholicism would be mine in time.

It is as inevitable as the seasons, as Lawrence began to see. *Accedit homo ad cor altum et exaltabitur Deus*. Ps. 63. Ask Eric to comment on this text.

We turned up the psalms. The Douai version had:

Man shall come to a deep heart, and God shall be exalted.

Gill was not really very good on this. He led the conversation off it and on to his own favourite figure in the psalms, 'the noonday devil'.

While we were out for a walk the following morning, Gill said that, although Fr D'Arcy was a delightful fellow, he [Gill] did not really care for the Jesuits. They had no roots in the true Christian world before the Council of Trent, which had spoilt everything. Gill described himself as a pre-Tridentine Christian. And, on the whole, he stuck to the Dominicans. Father Bernard was a Benedictine, but there had been an element of chance in that encounter.

On Saturday morning, Father Bernard was lucky and unlucky. He was lucky because he was allowed to take some of the Hague children to a *matinée* performance at the cinema in High Wycombe. He was unlucky because René Hague came to lunch and tormented him about it. Father Bernard had a passion for Donald Duck, to whom he referred familiarly as 'Donald' and whose adventures he delighted to recount.

On Palm Sunday, the Gills and their dependents went out to church, and there was no mass in the private chapel. I walked in the woods. They were alive with grey squirrels, and the hazel and the willow both had their catkins.

73

As a boy, I had always known the silver-furred willow catkins as 'palm', but the Gills came home with little strips of genuine, dried palm-leaf twisted and looped into the form of a cross, which they tucked into picture-frames or laid on their dressing-tables.

From Gill's publisher there came advance copies of a new book, *The Necessity of Belief*. In it, there was further play with the erotic analogies of mystical experience. Gill made (as Graham Greene tends to do) 'believe' an intransitive verb. There are, he implied, two kinds of temperament, the believing and the unbelieving, and the unbelieving are dreary.

If they can reject what you have to give, they will do so. They expect to be convinced by force or not at all. They cannot see that they must collaborate. They refuse to collaborate. They are like those virgins who can only be raped.

Clearly, I was one of these. Certainly, my conversion was now off, though it would leave me with a metaphysical hangover for years.

FOURTEEN

Back in London, I renewed contact with Murry. It was April. Towards the middle of the month, Herbert Read told me that I might be hearing from James Hanley, the proletarian novelist, who, having bought a derelict mansion in North Wales, had written to say that, with all this space, he would like to do something for a deserving young writer, if he, Read, knew anybody who was hard up and wanted peace in which to write.

Five letters came from Murry. The first had been written in mid-Atlantic. It hinted at difficulties of which I might have been unaware while I was staying at Larling last autumn. Then followed three letters with an elaborate heading printed in red, which indicated that the *communitas* had been formed as a limited company, whose directors were Murry himself, his brother Richard, Sir Richard Rees, the Marxist schoolmaster and a doctor in Norwich whom I remembered coming to tea at Larling. Max Plowman was not among them. There was a registered office in London. The Hon. Treasurer also had a London address. The Hon. Sec. could be written to at the Centre itself, The Oaks, Langham, near Colchester, Essex. It all looked extremely businesslike. The straight answer to a straight question turned out in the end to be that I should be welcomed at the Centre *as cook*.

The letter from Hanley came between the fourth and the fifth of Murry's letters. It invited me to stay 'as one of the family' for an indefinite period. I wrote back to say that I would like to come to Glan Ceirw for some weeks, then to Murry to say that I was promised elsewhere for two months, but would like to come to Langham after that. This was arranged, Murry requiring me to present myself at the Oaks by mid-July.

. . . You are the ultimate cook; a penultimate one will be found . . . Till then, I wish you quiet living and peace of soul.

Jo would be living in the flat while I was in Wales. She could, indeed, regard it as finally restored to her, since, when I left Hanley's, I should be going straight to Langham, where I should settle. Dylan, it seemed, had once more gone back to Wales, though he was as far from Corwen as he could very well be.

In Wales, there was sun. There was rain. There were local *eisteddfodau*. Hanley wrote. I wrote abortively. At a council house in Corwen, John Cowper Powys wrote. A Neanderthal man in technicolour, Powys was the most beautiful male human being I have seen. At a *gorsedd* meeting on a rainy field one Saturday afternoon in Corwen, they made him, to his enormous pleasure, a bard (he was not, of course, despite his name, a Welshman). I was writing a proletarian novel to be called *Grey Children*. Hanley later borrowed this title for a sociological work. At this time, he had done one Dai *bach* story, but was still writing mainly about the sea. Hanley, who had been a railway-porter at Bootle, was a gentle, tender-hearted man. If he shot a rabbit without killing it stone-dead, I had to break its neck, while he leaned his head on his arm against a tree-trunk.

I had the proofs of *Apology for Dancing*. Letters came. Letters were sent. Mussolini's gallant Fascist armies bombed and gassed their way through Abyssinia. Soon the two months of rustic pleasures were over, and it was time to go back to London and thence to the Adelphi Centre. Cooking looked easy. To cook for the new and better world might be fun. I sent a post-card to Jo

Atterbury to say that I should like to use the flat for ten days or so in early July. That would give me time to look round old haunts before I departed for Langham.

It would be the 7th or 8th of July 1936 when I returned from Corwen. I got to Mortimer Market in the late afternoon or early evening, I fancy about six o'clock. At any rate, the workpeople had packed up and gone, and I expected Jo to be there. She might have been kept at the office or she might have gone round to deliver a typescript at the house of a private client (for she did some literary and other typing). I was a bit tired, and I should have liked to wash the grit from behind my ears. I was also hungry. I'd hoped for a welcoming Jo with a cup of tea. I had no key. I sat on the stairs, nursing my rucksack.

I wondered if Jo was in fact inside, determined not to let me in. My sense of hearing is sufficiently acute, and I could detect no sound. I nevertheless had the notion that I was aware of somebody's presence in the flat. Then I decided that I would go out for a bite at some café. I would leave my rucksack here by the door. By the time I got back, Jo would very likely have come.

She had. There was some constraint in her manner. This might well be accounted for by my visible irritation and by reluctance to go and live at home again, even for ten days, after so protracted an enjoyment of the premises. There may even have been the fear that it would turn out to be longer than ten days.

I think I had better tell this story in full. It did not directly concern Orwell, but Jo Atterbury had been his girl, and, a few weeks afterwards, he heard the story from me. So I suppose it is part of the documentation of his life.

I duly revisited old haunts and saw all those of my friends who were in London. I completed the Sunday and Monday routines up to and including a *New English Weekly* gathering (alas, without Michael) in the Silver

Buffet of the Holborn Restaurant. That was Monday, 13th July.

When I reached Mortimer Market, Jo was again there. She was giving the flat a thorough clean, even shaking mats out of the window. In those days of comparatively little traffic and comparatively few wireless sets, even London was pervaded by the true summer languor. The evenings were peaceful. This was a bright, splendid evening. The hair on Jo's head was like corn-stubble. The round blue eyes behind her spectacles were as merry as they ever succeeded in being.

When Jo had gone, I saw that on the desk were half-a-dozen sheets of typing paper, covered with her hand-writing in green ink. It was not the first time she had left things lying about, sometimes intended as messages. There had been poems. There had been drawings, by some young commercial artist keeping his eye in, of herself in the nude (touching, because her body had a gross beauty). This was a story. The title was *Prelude to Poison*. The six sheets are here in front of me. I transcribe.

Her hand shook as she poured the China tea, its silky steam clinging to the glowing surface. She watched it writhe and curl – almost tangible. This is the last time you will look at a beautiful thing, the last time your faculties of appreciation will stir. Is tea an antitoxin to morphia? Perhaps she oughtn't to drink it? The last time – the last time.

The tube rattled – it was not full. Had the doctor missed it? Six months she had had it. Did poison keep its strength as long as that – she had been careful not to take the minute cork from the phial? Was there enough? – To screw your courage to the sticking point and then to fail? When fatal poisons were missed doctors kicked up a dust until they were reclaimed – perhaps the proportion of morphia in them was too negligible to matter – God, woman, don't be such a coward. Do it now, as the Wayside Pulpits say.

The thirteen tiny tablets trickled into her hand – she must use them now before the air absorbed their potency. What a fool she had been to come here – like Dostoievsky's criminals visiting the scene of the crime. Why hadn't she taken a single to Leeds, Bradford, Halifax, Huddersfield or Wakefield – wool towns of Yorkshire, forming a ring – ring – Yorkshire – Wakefield – haunting Wakefield? Hell, what are you dithering for, why are you wasting time? 'Ee, that's a bonny colour, lass' – blithering sentimentalist – get on with the job.

She wasn't leaving a note – all suicides do that – besides it might implicate someone, however detached she might make it. It wouldn't implicate him here, would it? No, it was too long ago – two months. It was an eternity to her, but perhaps, – was it to an outsider – to the person who found her, for instance? But then nobody knew who was likely to come here – it's perfectly all right – you're only making excuses to delay.

The tea had stopped steaming and was a clear golden brown – better not to have drunk it. Throw the tube onto the roof opposite – what more natural than a heart attack whilst taking a nice domestic cup o' tea? Quite cheerful when last seen by her office companion Miss M. who gave evidence at the P.M. Hell, they'd find the morphia then – but nobody knew the motive, thank God for that. Ought to have thought it out more carefully, though. Anyway, he'd never hear of it – he'd gone – gone – hollow word – she'd better swallow them all together in case they took effect too quickly and she didn't take enough – ought to have found out more about it – cowardice – she didn't really want to be sure there was enough – that would annihilate her only excuse.

She sat down and poured all the tablets into her mouth at once with a gesture of voluptuous satisfaction. She sat quite still for five minutes thinking idly – then she remembered the door – she got up – she was quite steady – how awful – perhaps it didn't work for hours. She went into the passage and pressed the catch up – only Patricia had a key and she was away for the weekend so she wouldn't be dropping in. She walked back to the chair – still steadily. Like sleep she did not know the moment of its coming. She leaned her head on her arms and settled herself comfortably – her limbs felt numb – or was that imagination – and drowsily she died.

*   *   *

Heavy footsteps resounded on the stairs. The glass rattled loosely in its socket under the impatient knuckles. The disused handle was thoughtlessly tried – of course not – self-contained unfurnished flat – own front door – he thought sarcastically – opulent suburbanites. He turned to go – then abruptly sat down on the stairs and puffed angrily at his reeking pipe – bloody well wait, now I have come all this way, he

At this point, the manuscript ends abruptly, without punctuation, without even a row of dots. Presumably, Jo had been interrupted by my entrance. Perhaps she had not intended to clean up this evening, but had either begun heaving things about in order to cover her embarrassment or (more likely) had already had the brushes and dusters out so that she could whip the story away and begin to clean when she heard my feet on the stairs. In that case, I had perhaps not been meant to see the story.

One of the people for whom Jo did occasional typing was a doctor. She *could* be carrying a tube of morphia tablets about with her. The ending made it seem likely that a soundless Jo *had* been in the flat when I returned from Corwen. Not that I ever smoked a pipe, reeking or not. Perhaps she had really thought of killing herself while I sat on the stairs, returning after, precisely, 'two months'. Perhaps she had actually measured out her thirteen tablets. If so, she had been very quiet about it.

The girl in the story had completed the operation. The more closely autobiographical the other details were, the safer that made it. Jo had been there, measuring out poison into a tea-cup, and had then poured it down the sink and decided to let me in. In that case, the danger was over.

If Jo had left the story as a message, its meaning would then be:

'This nearly happened. I wanted you to know.'

That it was called '*Prelude* to Poison' did suggest the usual lover's threat, but it might simply be Jo's idea of a neat title. There had been some thought for style. (Words have been crossed out. In the very first sentence, 'golden' has been substituted for 'glowing'. '*Tiny* tube.' 'Dangerous' instead of 'fatal'.) I was feeling pleasantly drunk. I concluded that there was perhaps something to worry about, but not much and not urgently.

No doubt Jo would look in again tomorrow. She would certainly be looking in before Saturday, when I went to Langham. I had better tax her with all this. I would also remind her that it was Huddersfield, not Wakefield.

That was Monday evening. On Wednesday morning, there was a knock at the door. It was a policeman.

'Excuse me, sir . . .'

'Come in,' I said.

'Thank you. It's about a Miss Atterbury, sir. Her mother reports she hasn't been home for two nights, where she was expected. It appears she sometimes stays here, sir.'

I explained.

'Have you seen Miss Atterbury lately, sir?'

I told the policeman that I had seen her on Monday evening and that I had then supposed she was on her way home.

'Any idea where she might be, sir?'

I had none at all, no. Miss Atterbury had a good many friends, and they were accustomed to put each other up at a moment's notice. Perhaps she just hadn't wanted to go home. She was over twenty-one, after all, and she'd spent a good deal of time away from home.

'. . . Would you like some coffee?'

'Well, not just now, sir. I must be off. Just a routine enquiry, you understand.'

'Yes, of course. Good morning.'

'Morning, sir.'

I had a visitor to tea in the afternoon, the dancer with whom I was supposed to be in love. We had strawberries. I told her about the policeman.

'. . . He clearly thought,' I said, 'that I was hiding a body under the bed, but, as you can see . . .'

There was a knock. I answered the door. Two middle-aged women stood on the stairs, rather tearful. They said they were looking for Jo. One of them was Mrs Atterbury. The other was Jo's aunt. I told them that I had already had a policeman and that I had seen Jo on Monday evening. She had left about nine o'clock. I had thought she was going home. No doubt she was staying with one of her office friends.

The older woman burst into tears, and the other said:

'She hasn't been to the office today or yesterday. We've just come from there.'

I clucked sympathetically, but did not feel that I could be expected to ask the two women in, what with my guest and the strawberries. They went. I returned to my guest.

'So you see?' I said.

When I had put my visitor on the 'bus, I rang Mabel up from a call box at Warren Street.

'Have you seen Jo?' I said.

'No, dear boy. Why?'

I told her, Mabel thought it very exciting. She supposed Jo must be wandering with loss of memory. I told her about the story on my desk. Well, then, said Mabel, it was obvious, they'd be finding Jo's body any day now. She'd committed suicide for love of me. What fun.

'You *are* a fool, Mabel, really.'

'Well!'

'It's damned annoying,' I said. 'She might have waited. I'm off to the Centre on Saturday, and I *must* know where my things are going to be.'

'Dump them here, dear boy.'

I went to Mabel's on Friday. The companion had, by then, had a letter with a Fishguard postmark. Jo was in bed. She had gone down by night train on Monday, taken a room at the first hotel she came to and swallowed her tablets. They had made her very sick. The companion was to tell me that I could keep whatever I wanted from the flat in Mortimer Market and either sell the rest or throw it away. I was not to hold myself in any way to blame. Jo would be continuing on her way and looking for a job in Dublin, where she would settle.

FIFTEEN

On Saturday, I ate a sandwich at Liverpool Street and caught a train just after midday, before the rush of homebound clerks had begun. In those days, it never occurred to me to buy a newspaper. If I had bought one for the journey that day, I should have gathered (nobody told me until weeks afterwards) that there was trouble in Spain. On Sunday night, a man called Calvo Sotelo had been shot. Now the military governor of the Canaries, a Gen. Francisco Franco, had flown to Morocco and issued a proclamation. It was 18th July 1936. The paper that Saturday would be in possession of the rumour that this Franco was about to invade or had already invaded the mainland, disembarking Moorish and Foreign Legion troops at Seville.

From Colchester, one took a 'bus seven or eight miles along the main Ipswich road and alighted a little way before Stratford St Mary's. A few miles away were Dedham, East Bergholt and the Constable country. Langham, reached by a left turning off the main road, was a widely scattered, undistinguished village in a pleasant but flat countryside. The Oaks was a big, square house, with extensive gardens, a field at the back and a well-grown gingko tree at the front. It had been built by a local girl who had made good in Edwardian London. During her later years, the house had witnessed many a jolly, bewhiskered orgy.

The people already there were living in Little Oaks, a kind of lodge to one side. A red-bearded sculptor of my acquaintance was there. So was another man with a beard, a non-practising architect who had once held the *Prix de Rome* and saw no reason for exerting himself again. His girl, a huge, delightful Canadian, worked very hard. So, I suppose, in a tortuous way all her own, did a wiry and intense little woman, a business man's wife from Liverpool. The office, in The Oaks proper, already functioned, and in it typed the Hon. Sec., an excitable little Scotswoman, very thin and bright-eyed and with orange hair. The doctor from Norwich sneered down his thin, pink nose into his moustache and made sly observations indicative of a belief in Original Sin.

The sculptor and Richard Murry were our practical men. Though a great deal of plaster-boarding went on upstairs, the main workshop was what was to become the lecture room. The sculptor set me to making a lectern.

That evening, there was a dance at the village hall. A local gentleman farmer had invited the nucleus round for drinks beforehand. Sitting about the floor or on the arms of chairs and the edges of tables, there were ex-Army-officer fruit-growers and their lean, smoking wives. But there was also a tall, fair girl I could not take my eyes off. She was, it appeared, the resident secretary of S. L. Bensusan, a Spanish-Jewish writer of Essex dialect stories, whose estate marched with The Oaks, and she came from Monmouthshire. For me, this was the *coup de foudre*. It was never seriously in doubt that I should, in due course, marry this young woman.

Up the lane was the Shepherd and Dog. Beyond the field at the back of The Oaks was a bird-sanctuary and, beyond that, the Bensusans' house. Bensusan's brother-in-law, Lucien Pissarro, painted much in the neighbourhood. His wife would drive him out in the morning, find him a subject, set up his easel and folding stool, make sure that he was comfortable and then drive away and collect him in time for lunch.

Apart from two splendid gardeners, Barrell and Byles,

the lower orders of the neighbourhood did not take kindly to us. Having concluded that we were nudists, they were disappointed to see so little and tended to throw stones. Their suspicions were probably based on the sculptor's red beard, the mousier one of the non-practising architect and the latter's sandals and shorts. From all I could gather, they had not taken kindly to the Bensusans either. They were not, perhaps, a kindly peasantry. The Shepherd and Dog was a very good pub, however, and the bearded architect's dart-playing stood us in good stead there. The architect had studied muscular co-ordination according to the principles of Matthias Alexander. He lay on his bed all day, practising muscular co-ordination and rolling cigarettes. In the evening, he played darts with impressive nonchalance and startling accuracy.

I did not much care for the general ambience at The Oaks and Little Oaks. I wrote to Max Plowman and begged him to come to Langham. I did not want to see Murry so quickly bogged down. Max's reply appears in the big volume of his letters called *Bridge into the Future*, without, however, any indication that the reference is to Murry. He wrote:

Yes. I know the 'kind of helplessness'. And it appeals like a glow-worm to the ungratified desire of the mother-hungry woman. There is in fact nothing more appealing to any socially-constituted person – let's add that, to save our face in confessing how much it appealed to the woman in me; but the jolt comes when the child who loves to hold a hand jumps up and says the spirit of Napoleon is upon him and he must now take Moscow – at once.

This was written on 24th July, three days before my twenty-fifth birthday. Max Plowman was holding back from the Centre and even, as far as the summer school went, meant only to come down and stay over Sunday night, 9th August, though he wondered whether he couldn't also 'somehow come down and hear you on the Wednesday', presumably the following Wednesday, the 12th. It had also been arranged that Murry and 'Col' should go for a week's holiday with the Plowmans 'directly the school is over'. Much (thought Max) would depend upon what happened during that week. Much, that is to say, with regard to the future of *The Adelphi* and so on. Rees, too, was contracting out. The holiday was to be on the Norfolk Broads.

Before the summer school began, there was an alarm which struck the rest of us as very amusing, though it can hardly have amused Murry at the time. Presumably, his three children were all at Langham, and presumably he believed that he had finally broken with Betty. The faithful and sweet-natured gardener, Hewitt (known as 'Bodge'), rang up one afternoon to announce to Murry that Betty had hired a fast car and was on her way to Langham to kidnap either all three children or just her own, the young Mary. I had gone back, after lunch, to work at my lectern when in panted the sculptor with this news. Little Oaks was being barricaded.

Murry then changed his tactics. He packed all three children into his car and drove off into the blue. As, however, he had prepared no rear position, he came back not very late in the evening. Betty had then been rampaging around for hours, tickled by the panic she had inspired. She was persuaded to go to bed and leave all till the morning. As, however, it was feared that she might get up and make a sudden pounce, I was posted in her room. I cannot be certain who posted me there. I assumed that I was doing what Murry wished, but, now that I come to think of it, the idea may have been the lady from Liverpool's. I sat at Betty's bedside and made what conversation seemed possible under the circumstances. It was mainly about the lady from Liverpool that Betty poured out her stream of picturesque obscenities. She seemed to assume that John ('the old bugger') had left her for this lady (a highly improbable notion). I felt, I must say, rather sympathetically disposed towards Betty, though the conversation itself was very boring. Eventually, I was relieved from my post. I will not state this as an incontrovertible fact, but I think that the following day all the Murrys drove up to London and went to see a solicitor, with the idea of getting some kind of agreement set out in legal form.

People assembled for the summer school. For the first session (a Saturday evening), S. L. Bensusan was invited to (and did) take the chair. Among the young women, a textile designer from somewhere in Lancashire, with a plump and charming figure and a bulging forehead, sang folksongs prettily, unaccompanied. An ancient poet declaimed his verse with a wild and vatic utterance. I drove around with an industrial chemist who worked on colloidal copper compounds for Boots'. He had written a novel, which he hoped Murry would help him to place (Murry did help him to place it, and the publisher cabled his offer from somewhere in mid-Atlantic). The colloidal chemist had a tenor voice on the operatic scale. One of the women had a soprano to match. Washing-up, though it might not save our souls, was delightful enough when these two were on it, with Mabel to put in her smaller *mezzo*, and Professor John Macmurray and me to combine on the bass.

Intellectually, Macmurray dominated that summer school in exactly the same way as, since the war, I have known another Scottish moral philosopher do elsewhere. Macmurray held a seminar each day after tea. His subject was what had happened to the Russian Revolution. According to Marx himself, the last country to go Communist should have been Russia. All the Marxian prophecies had gone wrong. In Russia, the Revolution was betrayed. We had our Marxists, led by the intellectual schoolmaster from Tooting, but they were a small and also a rather unpopular group. When they mentioned Russia, there were nasty remarks about Radek, which rather got in the way of their Popular Front canvassing and attempts to collect for Spain, where, I now gathered, a civil war raged.

'George Orwell' was coming down to give one of the morning lectures (using this name for serious things now, it seemed, not merely for his pot-boiling novels). Murry and I both independently had the idea that I ought to be Orwell's chairman. He duly came, and I was. After his lecture, the two of us withdrew to the Shepherd and Dog. We talked a great deal, but I do not think Spain was mentioned (it was four months later when Orwell went to Spain). The marriage had taken place two months before, on June 9th. Eric and Eileen would live at the village shop in Wallington, near Baldock, Hertfordshire. I told Eric Jo Atterbury's story. No reference was made to the rather spectacular set-to eight months ago. Inwardly, I recalled it without discomfort, though also without feeling that I should ever understand what it had all been about. The humorous afterthoughts and the residual puzzlement would be, if not exactly mutual, yet compatible. Orwell and I settled down to the position of old friends. The ideal frequency with which we should henceforward meet would be every few months.

At the summer school, there were few untoward incidents. One morning, dodging a lecture, the textile designer and I were dancing to the gramophone in a big room near the lecture room, to which one descended by a short flight of stairs. I do not think it occurred to either of us that the tune of our fox-trot would be audible to those at the lecture. Murry, however, came out of the lecture room, his brow like thunder, switched off the gramophone and went back again. He had been rather attentive to the textile designer, and we decided he was jealous.

Murry was not yet a pacifist. My lecture was not explicitly pacifist, but its trend lay that way. Its title was *Material or Spiritual Crisis?* It was against trying to force the movement of events. It suggested a kind of new monasticism, a withdrawal into the desert. At the end, the Marxists walked out as though in collective protest. After a pause, a plain-clothes parson stood up and said that there was really nothing to add except, 'God help us.' At that moment, a cow passing the windows bellowed loudly. Yet nobody laughed. Afterwards, Murry asked me to walk round a bit with him. He took my arm, and we walked at least two miles. He did not say a word. If it comes to that, neither did I.

That is how I remember the occasion. The audience had, I should have said, been spellbound. My wife (not yet my wife) was present and assures me that that was in fact the case. However, she no doubt was a prejudiced witness. Murry wrote in his diary:

Rayner gave an embarrassing lecture last night, which made me so acutely ashamed for him that I could not look at his face while he delivered it. Afterwards, he sought me out in the garden at Little Oaks, and we walked along the road together arm in arm in silence: and that was good.

I am prepared to distrust my memory. Still, there was a peculiarity about Murry's ability to look, or not look, at other people's faces. The Lea biography quotes a passage in which he claimed that he did not meet people's eyes because he feared to discover in their faces that *they* were telling lies – an original, though not, for that reason, necessarily a wrong notion. In fact my lecture anticipated a number of ideas and actual phrases which Murry himself adopted in his ensuing pacifist phase.

He came back a pacifist from the Norfolk Broads holiday with Plowman. I very well remember his return. I had just begun to function as 'the ultimate cook' and was quite enjoying it. On 6th September his diary records that, while he hesitates to be sanguine, it certainly does appear that I have found my true *métier*. This, he says, would be the 'glorious justification' of a hunch imparted, when she was over in May, to the American woman whom I had better call Hetty. I do not know what her surname is now. At one time, she had been married to a doctor and Adlerian psychiatrist who had intermittently seemed to be living at Richard Rees's. Murry and she had known each other for quite a long time, but had only fallen into each other's arms at a hotel in New York earlier in the year, in circumstances which Hetty later described to me in abominable detail.

With the departure of the summer visitors, the permanent nucleus had moved into the big house. Murry himself occupied Little Oaks. Hetty appeared there. She was small and dark, a clever woman of great charm, tough and experienced, though not unfeminine. Murry's private life became too complicated. He took to spending the week at Larling and coming to Langham for the week-end, when there were frequently visitors. This suited neither Hetty nor Betty.

Richard Rees had gone. First, he took up painting. Then he went off to Spain, driving ambulances. Rees had financed *The Adelphi*. Now it was to be reorganized for subscribers only. There was talk of me being editor. There was talk of printing the paper ourselves, and printing apparatus was in fact set up in a room at Little Oaks. S. L. Bensusan's secretary came to live at the Oaks. By a manoeuvre on the part of James Hanley, I found myself sitting on the British executive committee of the International Association of Writers for the Defence of Culture, which involved going to London. The meetings were held at a historic house in Hampstead, under the chairmanship, first, of Lascelles Abercrombie, then of Cecil Day Lewis.

Among those present would be Rose Macaulay and Rosamund Lehmann. At one point, Stephen Spender was in the midst, but that was somewhere other than in Hampstead and must hve been after we had joined forces with an organization called For Intellectual Liberty. I could not think why I was there. I contributed nothing to the discussions, though at one point I made an into-the-desert speech at a public meeting. It did not go down at all well.

Hetty finally adopted as her mission teaching the facts of life to a young Welsh poet, a Catholic convert, who liked older women and eventually went off with one of them. Before that, she had taken to coming over to my room with a bottle of the 1929 Côtes de Bourg from Murry's cellar at Little Oaks. We would drink this and talk about Murry's wickedness and what a lovely person Max Plowman was. We both thought Max Plowman a lovely person, and I was becoming more and more anti-Murry. I cannot remember precisely why this was, but I do know that I started writing a book about St Paul, which was really a book *against* St Paul, the short man with a terrible will to power and a down on women. St Paul was Murry, and I rather saw Max Plowman in the role of St Stephen. I concluded, I know, that Murry, despite all appearances to the contrary, was a cold man and that, like a vampire, he fed on Max's emotional warmth.

One appearance to the contrary, whose precise occasion I do not recall, took place in the sitting-room at Little Oaks. It may have been that I had agreed not to go up to London on a day when Murry wanted me not to go up to London. At any rate, I had, exceptionally, pleased him.

He ducked his head sideways, rushed at me, folded me in his arms and started going over me with little nibbling kisses, saying:

'Dear old boy, dear old boy, dear old boy, dear old boy . . .'

I don't remember thinking this particularly odd. That is to say, it was an odd way to *behave*, and I found it rather embarrassing, if only because there was nothing for me to do except stand there, but I didn't think there was anything odd *behind* it or that Murry's state of mind was at all unusual.

On another occasion, when I was in bed with flu, he came into my room just after breakfast and, standing over me, told me that I had denied my essence and that salvation was after the flesh. Even at the time, I did not quite understand in what way I had denied my essence, though denying one's essence was clearly a frightful thing to do, like committing a sin against the Holy Ghost. That salvation was after the flesh had something to do with a tendency I still showed to toy with Christian notions of an immortal soul.

The hunch about my cooking had proved false. On 16th November Murry's diary laconically says:

Langham on Friday: faced by a domestic crisis over Rayner's cooking.

A week before, however, there had been trouble. I quote two of Murry's journal entries in full.

Nov. 8. 1936. I saw Margery was in a bad way because of what is happening between [Hetty] and Rayner; and I had to make Margery see the thing as (I believe) it ought to be seen. And in doing this, the virtue does go out of one. To persuade people not to judge – to let individuals be – is very hard.

Nov. 9. 1936. Rayner, yesterday, informed me that he proposed to go to America on January 8 (i.e. with [Hetty]); I assured him that he would not be letting me down.

Margery was the thin and excitable Scottish secretary. Poor soul, she did not long survive her dreadful experiences at Langham. Once, certainly, pretty and of a positively Heaven-sent warm-heartedness and quick responsiveness of nature, I suppose that a disappointment in love had somehow left her stranded. The really frightful thing is that, while everybody was fond of her, the preoccupied people she had to do with always sooner or later found her a bit of a nuisance or an embarrassment (and experienced sensations of guilt in consequence, according to their capacities for guilt). It looks, from Murry's diary here, as though she supposed there to be more between Hetty and me than there was. I suppose that she feared for my future wife, about whom she would even try to excite me, expatiating on her beauty as she stepped out of the bath.

As to me telling Murry that I meant to go to America with Hetty, I hardly know what to make of this, I have no memory of the occasion and cannot say whether I ever in fact thought of going to America with Hetty. Perhaps she wanted me to go, and perhaps I wanted to go to America. Perhaps it was part of an attempt on Hetty's part to make Murry jealous, and perhaps I (who was certainly on her side and would have liked Murry to settle for her) played either a conscious or an unconscious accomplice's part. Perhaps I was simply trying to needle Murry. I don't know.

Certainly, I meant to leave the Centre after Christmas. On 20th December Murry records that I told him as much. On the same date, he quotes me as contradicting myself on the question of the lack of respect of one individual for another. He adds, as though I were some kind of invalid:

Yet I can't help liking Rayner: I should like to do something to help him. But *que faire*? Otto, Rayner and I put together the chicken coops.

On 7th January 1937 occurs the entry:

At a governors' meeting it was decided that Rayner must leave.

But I had already gone.

At the end of February, I was married at Hampstead Town Hall. Our witnesses were Max Plowman and Herbert Read (who still owes us a picture we were to have had as a wedding present). The Macmurrays did a rather specially nice thing. I had run into John Macmurray two or three days before in Glenloch Road, Hampstead, where I had taken a room. It seemed he lived just round the corner. I told him I was getting married on Saturday, and he said he would like to give us a party. So what was arranged was that my wife and I should invite our friends to his flat and go round ourselves late on Saturday afternoon, when all would be ready. The Macmurrays would then go out, returning later as guests and ringing the doorbell. They laid on everything, including caviare.

Both Plowman and Murry had opposed the marriage. In Max's case, this was for my sake. In Murry's, it was for my wife's. Max thought poets should be unconfined by bonds in which he had 'bumped for twenty-five years'. Murry told S. L. Bensusan's former secretary that I should make her suffer, since I was egocentric like himself.

For the time being, my wife went on living at the Centre. I went down at week-ends when I had the fare. I was still decidedly at loggerheads with Murry, who was also at loggerheads with himself. The permanent nucleus, too, were all at loggerheads with one another. No doubt it was the lack of any real common purpose. Whatever they might pretend, everybody was there for private reasons, usually connected with some previous failure. I had no quite specific quarrel with Murry.

A harsh and irrevocable moment occurred at the Easter school. I was there only to see my wife. Bored and irritated by a lecture, which I had remembered as Murry's but which, from Murry's diary entry for the date, 31st March 1937, was in fact by Max Plowman on 'The Necessity of God' with Murry as chairman, I went out and drank by myself at the Shepherd and Dog. When I got back, the discussion was still going on.

The colloidal chemist was on his feet, a big, brown-faced man with a French-type moustache and bobbed black hair (he tells me this is now white). His novel, called *Sugar in the Air*, had been made a Book Society choice. He had begun a second novel, *Asleep in the Afternoon*, in part a satirical portrait of the Centre and its inhabitants (I seem to figure as two characters in it). He was now making a speech which ended with the words 'to make gods in one's own image'.

Murry was ruffled by this, to begin with.

'Who,' he said from the platform in hurt tones, 'is making gods in his own image?'

This cue, alas, I found irresistible.

'Well, you,' I said, 'have been earning your living at it these . . .'

And, as I recall (and as Murry's diary confirms), I said 'thirty years', which was fifteen too many.

This produced nothing but an anguished:

'Rayner . . .!'

And my mood was such that I did not even feel sorry. I do now.

Upstairs, J. W. N. Sullivan was dying in a wheeled chair. Before Hetty left, I had met her in London to take Sullivan to a consultation with an neurologist. An operation at the base of the skull was recommended, which might give Sullivan fifteen years of life. He declined it. According to Hetty, who was an out-and-out psycho-somaticist, Sullivan had paralysed himself by his determination, after the birth of a child, to become impotent, because he hated his wife. Murry, whose association with Sullivan went back at least to the early days of *The Adelphi*, had invited him to settle at the Centre. He lived in his wheeled chair in a large room on the first floor. Murry had a good collection of recordings of Beethoven's late string quartets. Every now and then, somebody would go up to Sullivan's room, get out a new set of records and change the needle. A mathematician, Sullivan was most widely known for a book on Beethoven.

My wife was to leave the Centre about a week after my dreadful intervention, but there was some delay because of the first manifestation of a medical crisis which blew up later. I am at fault for not recalling that it was partly Max Plowman whom I had seemed to attack (I never did recall it, even very shortly afterwards). I claim a very little, not intellectual but human, credit for also not recalling that I was given some cue for hitting back. Murry records:

I could not, though maybe wrongly, refrain from describing him

– *i.e.*, me, for 'the spirit in which [I] spoke was truly horrible' –

as 'a specialist in God.' . . . Then he took a savage cut at me . . .

I continue with the quotation.

I felt, and feel, that I have had quite enough of R. H. *J'en ai soupé*. I would like to have done with him for ever. He is like the pariah dog that will always bite the hand that feeds it – I do *not* mean mine; actually, it was his treatment of Max that angered me. Yet, alas, the moment I say that I want to have done with him, I feel that I may have to begin all over again, by trusting him more than ever. And as always I don't feel a bit good about this. If I do it will be quite in spite of myself; and I foresee much trouble.

Four or five days later, he is still intending to write and ask me to go back to the Centre and edit *The Adelphi*. It was my wife who discouraged him from this course. I did not know, or I might have made a fuss.

The Adelphi Centre, as such, had no second summer school. It fell increasingly into Peace Pledge Union hands and became, for a while, a home for Basque refugee children. Murry went back to Larling and tried to arrange a *modus vivendi* with Betty. For a while, the Prix de Rome architect, now married, settled at Little Oaks. I liked his wife, and he and I so far composed our differences that I stayed with him there. Max Plowman took over editorship of *The Adelphi*, as, with Rees, he had once done years before. I had contrived to upset him, too. Only recently have I quite seen how. I would not have offended him for worlds. I saw him only twice thereafter. My connection with *The Adelphi* ceased altogether.

SIXTEEN

I took the top floor of a house in Lisburne Road, which lies in the red brick back-end of Hampstead, towards Gospel Oak. My wife joined me on a Sunday. On Monday morning, she was in hospital, with a serious operation imminent. It was the Middlesex Hospital. The operation was, I fancy, on Tuesday. It was early April and already hot. The afternoon of the operation, just before closing time, I went to the Wheatsheaf in Rathbone Place to give myself Dutch courage. There I found Dylan Thomas, whom I had not seen for a year. With him was his own future wife, Caitlin. I had not met her before, and my first impression was how extraordinarily alike the two were. It was a resemblance which photographs do not bear out, perhaps never did. Dylan always had a putty nose and Caitlin, perhaps, always a beaky one, but Caitlin's features became more finely drawn later. In 1937, one thought her simply plump and rosy, her yellow hair a tangle about her shoulders. I seem to have gone in for coincidences of date. This was also the day *Sebastian* came out.

A few weeks later, I took my wife to Cornwall to pick up strength. Dylan and Caitlin appeared there, too. They were at a guest house called the Lobster Pot in Mousehole. Off Mousehole lay a small island, once, it was said, occupied by a hermit. After an evening's drinking in Lamorna, we came down over the hill when a huge, brilliant moon lay over this island, its light reflected with only the faintest tremor in the still waters of the bay. The splendour of the spectacle infuriated Dylan, who made savage remarks about picture-postcards and visual *clichés*.

I also recall a morning occasion in a sunny field above Newlyn. Dylan was carrying around with him and intermittently sipping from a flagon of 'champagne wine tonic', a Penzance herbalist's highly intoxicating brew sold very cheaply and without licence. Dylan talked copiously, then stopped.

'Somebody's boring me,' he said. 'I think it's me.'

At about this time, the Stalinists in Barcelona were systematically exterminating their Trotskyite and anarcho-syndicalist allies. Orwell, who had joined the P.O.U.M. forces, was there. So was Eileen. She was working in the I.L.P. office in Barcelona. I had a letter from Orwell in July, when my wife and I were back at Lisburne Road.

We started off by being heroic defenders of democracy and ended by slipping over the border with the police panting on our heels. Eileen was wonderful, in fact actually seemed to enjoy it. But though we got ourselves out all right, nearly all our friends are in jail . . . The most terrible things were happening even when I left, wholesale arrests, wounded men dragged out of hospital and thrown into jail, people crammed together in filthy dens where they have hardly room to lie down, prisoners beaten and half starved, etc. etc.

Adherents of the Popular Front in Britain played down these feuds on the republican side in Spain. Orwell had, he said, 'had a most amusing time with *The New Statesman*' on this account.

As soon as I got out of Spain I wired from France asking if they would like an article and of course, they said yes, but when they saw my article was on the suppression of the P.O.U.M. they said they couldn't print it. To sugar the pill they sent me to review a very good book which appeared recently, *The Spanish Cockpit*, which blows the gaff pretty well on what has been happening. But once again when they saw my review they couldn't print it as it was 'against editorial policy'.

Early that year, the publisher of *Down and Out in Paris and London* and of Orwell's three novels had issued *The Road to Wigan Pier* in Left Book Club limp orange covers.

As soon as he heard I had been associated with the P.O.U.M. and Anarchists and had seen the inside of the May riots in Barcelona, he said he did not think he would be able to publish my book, though not a word of it was written yet . . . However, I have two other publishers on my track and I think my agent is being clever and has got them bidding against one another. I have started my book, but of course my fingers are all thumbs at present.

He was back at Wallington. In Spain, he had been wounded.

My wound was not much, but it was a miracle it did not kill me. The bullet went clean through my neck but missed everything except one vocal cord, or rather the nerve governing it, which is paralysed. At first I had no voice at all, but now the other vocal cord is compensating and the damaged one may or may not recover. My voice is practically normal but I can't shout to any extent. I also can't sing but people tell me this doesn't matter. I am rather glad to have been hit by a bullet because I think it will happen to us all in the near future, and I am glad to know that it doesn't hurt to speak of.

Here I had better add that the wound did not permanently affect Orwell's voice, as has been widely supposed. That odd, thin voice had always been his. I ought perhaps also to add that, apart from what I have quoted, which was fair comment, there occurred in this letter mildly paranoiac suggestions about both the publisher and *The New Statesman*. Further villainy was ascribed to the latter for offering to pay for the review they did not print, an offer, usual from any reputable paper, which Orwell described as 'hush money'. The publisher was credited with having known beforehand what to expect when Orwell went to Spain and with having for that reason made a contract with him only to publish his works of fiction. There is also, here, some contradiction between Orwell's account of his dealings with publishers and the one to be found both in Christopher Hollis's book and the autobiography of Frederic J. Warburg, who indeed finally published *Homage to Catalonia*. Both claim that Orwell went out to Spain on a publisher's advance, whose amount, indeed, Warburg precisely states. Warburg has since checked up on the date of the contract and admits he was wrong.

Dylan Thomas and Caitlin were staying in Hampstead at the house of Anna Wickham, herself a poet, a big, ferocious-looking woman, with a blackhead-pitted brown face and rugger stockings. When drunk, she was reputed to bite people's heads and try to pull other women's breasts off. In the end, she hung herself out of her bedroom window, a curiously exhibitionist proceeding (unless, of course, she had been unable to find a big enough drop elsewhere). I remember the house as being at the top of Parliament Hill Road, just opposite where Orwell had been living when I first knew him, but it may have been in one of the other red brick streets nearby. The Thomases, with Anna, came down to Lisburne Road, which is moderately squalid. At the end, we had a Baptist chapel and, round the corner, a chemist's, a sweetshop and a 24 bus stop (at the other end, one quickly reached an iron bridge over a railway, across which lay Parliament Hill Fields). Caitlin lost her shoe in the street by the bus stop. She was prone to little misadventures of this kind. It was generally suspected that their purpose was to attract attention to herself or to break up some conversation in which she had no part. Temperamentally, I always felt (although Caitlin and I never had a cross word) that she had a great deal in common with Betty Murry. If it comes to that, I never directly had cross words with Betty Murry.

The interior colour-scheme of the house in Lisburne Road was remarkable. The walls were painted with dark, blue-green varnish paint. The woodwork was plum-coloured. To heighten the effect, the street-door panels and the skylight over our landing were of rose-tinted glass, so that strong sunlight poured through them a light at once altar-like and subaqueous. Our rooms were in fact one room and a kitchen, the kitchen big enough to eat in. In the front room were a single divan bed, a little chair once Jo Atterbury's, my desk and a chair which not only let down and could be made up as a bed but also had an extensible arm on which one could write (I am writing on it now) and bookshelves at both sides. This had been our principal wedding present. A solicitor in Newport (Mon.) had invited us to order any piece of furniture we liked and have the bill sent to him. We had gone to Heal's and chosen the most compendious piece we could find, with the idea that, if we were ever evicted, we should be able to set up house with it in the middle of the road. Sleeping in it felt like sleeping in a coffin, and so it was simply referred to as the coffin. The floors were stained black. The curtains were of a crude, unbleached stuff we had bought from the Malta tourist-publicity shop in Leicester Square.

In November, Richard Rees, who had returned from ambulance-driving with Julian Bell on the Madrid front and was living in Upper Park Road, had the American thinker and novelist, Waldo Frank, in tow. On 2nd December he gave a small party to which Orwell, having now finished *Homage to Catalonia*, came.

A dated appearance of Orwell in Lisburne Road was on 17th January 1938. He came unexpectedly and stayed to supper. After supper, he and I went out drinking and ended up in a Soho basement from which we returned between one and two o'clock in the morning. While my wife and I, a yard or two away, huddled together on the narrow divan, Orwell slept in the coffin. An hour or so later, pyjamaless, he had to get up for the usual reason. My wife remembers waking to see, in the dim light from a street lamp, against the shiny, dark-green-painted walls, the tall, bony figure of our guest padding, naked but for his little moustache, out of the room and presently back again.

My own clearest memory of that night is of confidences at the bar-counter. Orwell had concluded (whether by any systematic means and with medical confirmation, I do not know) that he was biologically sterile. He badly wanted children and was miserable about it. Then he became involved with a tart, and I had to rescue him. That was an exceptionally sunny January. It is noted that on the afternoon of the 17th I had walked in Ken Wood and seen my first jay.

I went to Wallington on 15th February, travelling by a Green Line bus which reached Baldock at a quarter past four. This was a Tuesday. The Stores was not a pretty cottage, and the village seemed desolate. There were two goats in a stinking shed at the back, and the Blairs rented a strip of ground, across the road at the front and above road-level, in which they grew vegetables and in which Eric and I dug together. He and Eileen behaved with conspicuous affection, fondling each other and sitting, if not on each other's knees, at any rate in the same armchair. The following winter, Eric went to Morocco, and Jack Common, former assistant editor of *The Adelphi*, borrowed the cottage at Wallington.

SEVENTEEN

At some point in 1938, I noticed that Murry was announcing in *The Times* that he would no longer be held responsible for his wife's debts, which I took to be a formal preliminary to divorce proceedings. A bit later, I saw and cut out from either one of the Sunday papers or *The News Chronicle* an article about him, with a photograph clearly some years out of date. The heading was:

THE MAN WHO CAME BACK TO GOD.

Murry, it seemed, was about to become a clergyman. His name had been entered at Westcott House theological college, Cambridge. He was to undergo an operation in February, and, if that was successful, to be ordained vicar 'of one of the most remote and poorest villages in England'. Evidently Betty had had a second child.

In the chintz drawing-room of his big house in the tiny village of Larling, near Thetford, Norfolk, with the soft cry in the background of his baby son being put to bed in another room, The Man Who Thought He Had Gone Beyond God told me last week . . .

It was apparently Hitler who had effected the change in Murry's outlook. Hitler was Antichrist. Organized religion was needed as a bulwark against the State. As the interviewer was leaving:

'I don't know what D. H. Lawrence, one of my most intimate and strangest friends, would have thought of me now if he were alive,' added Mr Murry with a smile.

That year, I saw Eric Gill either once or twice. I took my wife to Pigotts to tea, we being at that time in the neighbourhood. I remember nothing of the occasion except that the painter David Jones (author, also, of *In Parenthesis*) was there and that (inconsiderately, I thought) he put a match to the sticks in the open fire, which burned out, so that the fire would have to be laid again. It must have been between-seasons, and perhaps there was a chill in the air. Thereafter, I saw Gill only once more, either that year or the next, at some politico-literary party held in huge premises somewhere in London.

There was a lot of poetic activity in the winter of 1938–9. First, there was Tambimuttu from Ceylon, starting *Poetry (London)*. Then there appeared a number of poets from Scotland and the North, who were bringing out a magazine called *Seven* and who were out to create an apocalyptic movement based on a misunderstood text from Berdyaev. They were mildly in favour of me, but Dylan Thomas was to be their *chef d'école*. Dylan was living at Laugharne. At the top of the cliff, he said (in a letter, I suppose, for I did not see him at this time), was Richard Hughes the novelist in a castle, while he and Caitlin lived in a shed at the bottom (the shed being Hughes's). Discussing Dylan with a teetotal compatriot of his, just about then, I remember urging the view that what the compatriot would only admit to be Dylan's feck-lessness in fact made him a kind of modern St Francis. But I also felt that Dylan was stuck as a poet, that the development which should have happened hadn't and that, unless his talent now suddenly broadened, it would have been better he should die young, as, indeed, one could argue, he had long shown every sign of meaning to do.

That was early in 1939. Six weeks after the outbreak of the expected war, I received the oddest communication from Laugharne. Dylan Thomas, of all people, was, of all things, trying to get up a writers' manifesto against war. He had already written round to a number of our contemporaries. Our 'statements' were to be printed in some 'widely circulated popular literary magazine such as *Life and Letters*'. 'Join the Army,' said Dylan, 'and see the next world.' Until very shortly before the outbreak of war, I should have described myself as a pacifist, though I had now abandoned the position. Dylan, so far as I knew, had never been interested in large public matters, and I am afraid that I privately interpreted his communication as a sudden display of panic at the thought that he, too, might be called up. I did not say this. My reply must, all the same, have contained some indication of raised eyebrows, for it unfuriated Dylan.

His further letter is dated 2nd November 1939. Foolishly, I had been a bit pompous myself. I had spoken of it perhaps being the writer's duty to undergo contemporary reality at its most extreme. Dylan pounced on this.

When you come to talk about one's duty as a writer, then *one* can only say that his duty is to write. If to undergo contemporary reality to its most extreme is to join in a war . . . against people you do not know, and probably to be killed or maimed, then one can only say flippantly that the best poems about death were always written when the poets were alive, that Lorca didn't have to be gored before writing a bullsong, that for a writer to undergo the utmost reality of poverty is for him to starve to death and therefore to be, as a writer, useless . . . The matey folk-warmth of the trenches can only make for hysterical friendships, do or die companionships, the joking desperate homosexual propinquity of those about to die: the joy of living and dying with a Saturday football crowd on an exploding ground.

It was better, thought Dylan, to join the Ministry of Information, and 'receive a good salary for muddling information, censoring news, licking official stamps, etc., than it is to kill or be killed for a shilling, or less, a day'. Then the sun came out, and the tone of the end of the letter was friendly and personal.

When Dylan came to London in December, he had grown fat. He had also developed an outward cast in his eyes. It was almost a change of personality. The cast in his eyes seemed to diminish if not disappear altogether later, but from now on Dylan would be the baggy, oddly shaped man most people remember.

He was also gloomy. No longer taking a stand against the war, he yet seemed a prey to some large resentment. He was unable to write. He was hard up. His world did not suit him. He felt depressed. And all this was unjust. As we stumbled through the blackout in Rathbone Place, he said he and Caitlin did not deserve to be stuck in this way, because they were both 'hard-living people'. This was the only time I heard Dylan Thomas praise himself. He was now twenty-five, and this may have been the time of his real crisis, though, as much as three years before, his name had come up in conversation between myself and the editor of the *Life and Letters* Dylan so quaintly thought 'popular' and 'widely circulated'.

This editor had said, about Dylan's drinking:

'But why does he do it? Why is he so afraid of life?'

Dylan had got a copy of my novel, *The Blaze of Noon*, to review, either for *Life and Letters* or for *the New English Weekly*. At some midday meeting in the York Minster ('the French pub') he told me he kept hating the book for one reason or another, only to find that it had been written with so much self-consciousness that somewhere in the text he would find all his criticism anticipated. I do not think he ever did his review.

In early 1940 Orwell appeared, lamenting his medical

unfitness for the Army. I had in my keeping a Leica camera, with which I took photographs of him, later sending them to him for use in some American *Who's Who*. I was then living in St John's Wood, in more luxury than heretofore.

Eileen was working at, I think, one of the ministries. On 11th April, Orwell was still at Wallington.

I'm here alone, Eileen coming down at weekends when she can. They are working her to death in that office and I want to get her out of it if possible, but at present nothing is transpiring about a job for me. I haven't touched my novel . . . I am aiming to raise six cwt. of potatoes against the famine I foresee next winter.

What novel? *Coming Up For Air* was already out.

Two days later, I was able to announce the birth of a daughter. I quote the beginning of Orwell's letter for its tone.

Thousands of congratulations on the kid. I hope and trust both are doing well. Please give Margaret all the best and my congratulations. What a wonderful thing to have a kid of one's own, I've always wanted one so. But, Rayner, don't afflict the poor little brat with a Celtic sort of name that nobody knows how to spell. She'll grow up psychic or something. It took me nearly thirty years to work off the effects of being called Eric.

Orwell's dislike of his own name is an odd thing. I should have thought 'Eric Blair' as good a name as 'George Orwell'. Other people have managed to survive being called 'Eric' (I suppose the association is *Eric, or Little by Little*, which can mean little except to public school men), and I dare say as many have had trouble with 'George'. Perhaps Orwell would have had trouble with 'George' if it had been his real name. He may have objected to 'Blair' because it was said to be a Scottish name, the family never having thought of itself as even remotely Scottish. I do not know whether 'George' had appealed to him ('Orwell', of course, is an East Anglian river) as a working-class or as a royal name. I suspect the latter. He went on to say:

If I wanted a girl to grow up beautiful I'd call her Elizabeth, and if I wanted her to be honest and a good cook I'd choose something like Mary or Jane. The trouble is that if you called her Elizabeth everyone would think you'd done it after the queen, as she presumably will be some day.

I do not know whether I had said in my letter that I thought of giving my daughter the sort of name he called 'Celtic' or whether he had simply thought it the kind of thing I was liable to. I must have toyed with Welsh names. The child's mother was Welsh.

Orwell's candid and touching envy was expressed to her in terms reminiscent of D. H. Lawrence when, a week or two later, he bent over the clothes basket in which the child slept in the garden. He said how wonderful it must be to see a living being sprung from one's own loins.

EIGHTEEN

From Mary Murry, I gather that Eric Gill was at Langham, for a Peace Pledge Union conference, at Easter in 1940. She remembers that he went round with John and herself to the Shepherd and Dog. Almost at once thereafter, he was ordered to bed with what was variously described by his doctor as 'flu, German measles and congestion of the lungs. In bed, he wrote much of his autobiography. It came out towards the end of the year, while the bombs rained down on London and I, in Wiltshire, where I had put my wife and daughter for the duration, waited for my Army call-up papers. I think (but cannot be certain) that I read the book then, before my papers came. I remember noticing how the trick of putting words unnecessarily in inverted commas had grown on its author. I did not think the book quite first-rate. At about that time, Gill died after an operation for lung cancer. I did not know. Not until some time in 1943 did I in fact learn that Eric Gill was dead, and until a few months ago I had gone on supposing that it was in 1943 he died.

A few weeks after his death, I was called up and went off to a regiment of field artillery in Northern Ireland, where I spent the first sixteen months of a four-and-a-half years' military career equally without danger, merit and interest. It was a long, uneasy dream, from which every now and then I awoke to go on leave in Wiltshire or London. My family had reality. So had my few contacts with the world of writers in which I liked to recall that I had once been a free agent.

My first leave from Ireland was in April 1941. With a

friend on leave from the Navy, I went into the Swiss pub in Old Compton Street, Soho. There was Dylan sitting at a table with a girl I did not know.

He stood up, a look of awful misery on his face, and said:

'O God, Rayner, I haven't seen you for all this time, and now I'm too drunk to talk to you.'

That he was drunk had not been apparent until he stood up. Now he pitched forward, and, if there had been room, he would have fallen flat on his face. My companion and I caught him and restored him to the chair on which he had been sitting.

I ran into Dylan on several brief London visits during the war. He was apparently working for a documentary film company with its headquarters in Golden Square. I recall nothing that passed, except that, late one evening, on the way either to or from the Café Royal or the Coffee An', on hearing one of the party complain of feeling terrible, Dylan said:

'What you got, boy? Mice?'

I fancy the complainer was a Canadian poet who had recently got his ticket and whom I had earlier been accustomed to see on Saturday evenings in Belfast. He was later much befriended by Orwell and wrote one absolutely first-rate paragraph about him.

Orwell worked in the Indian section of the B.B.C.'s Overseas Service and later became literary editor of *Tribune*. He was at the B.B.C. while he was writing *Animal Farm*, that is, all through 1943. At 200 Oxford Street, he had the company of William Empson, the poet and language theorist, who worked in the Chinese section. This was great good luck for the war years, when there were so few writers in London and at liberty and one could not always choose one's company. I got three days' leave from the village near Doncaster where my unit was then stationed to give a talk for Orwell, on contemporary American short-story writers, in a series in which Herbert Read introduced the speakers. This was on 12th March 1943. By August, Orwell had had enough of the B.B.C. I (then in Lincolnshire) must have taxed him with cynicism on some point, for he replied:

You'd be cynical yourself if you were in this job. However I am definitely leaving it, probably in about three months. Then sometime in 1944 I might be near-human again and able to write something serious. At present I'm just an orange that's been trodden on by a very dirty boot.

From Febrary 1944, as a result of being medically down-graded from A1 to C2, I found myself generally in civilian billets, from which I was able to do a good deal of reviewing for *Tribune*. One thing Orwell editorially put me up to was Scot-baiting.

Reviewing an American book on the period, I evidently found occasion to describe the alignment of intellectuals here during the Spanish War. Orwell wanted me to delete certain references on the ground that, for instance, T. S. Eliot now worked for the British Council and had 'written at lease once for *British Ally*, the British propaganda paper published in Moscow', while Roy Campbell had become 'definitely anti-Fascist'. 'You might find other instances,' he said. 'e.g. Arthur Bryant.' When I enquired who this was, he explained:

Arthur Bryant is one of the big guns of the Conservative intelligentsia. He was the one who said during the Spanish War that 'the sawing off of a Conservative tradesman's legs is a common-place in republican Spain', a phrase which stuck in my memory.

What I then regarded as editorial caginess struck me as uncharacteristic of Orwell. I had also been disconcerted to see him, in *Partisan Review*, attacking pacifists. Orwell, too, had been taken up in what were to me, in my ignorance, unexpected quarters.

While I was in Ireland, I wrote a sequence of character sketches of the men in my hut. It was meant to be amusing, was done in a vein of exasperated affection and bore the title, ironically (if it needs to be said) intended, *I Am Not in Favour of the Working Classes*. I sent this to *Horizon* and received from its editor, Cyril Connolly, a note of rejection in which he said that he was sorry I was doing so badly in the Army but that he felt I did not really understand the working classes. As a guide, he recommended that I should read *The Road to Wigan Pier* by George Orwell. I did not know that Orwell and Connolly had been at the same prep. school and so, also, were 'old friends'.

That summer, the Blairs adopted a son, Richard Horatio, born about 11.00 a.m. on 14th May, as Orwell made a point of finding out in order that I might cast the child's horoscope (a parlour trick I had picked up during the last year of peace). I suppose he was named after Sir Richard Rees, then engaged in *liaison* with the French Navy.

From Murry I had once heard, while I was in Ireland. Still bent on freeing himself from Betty, he wrote to ask whether, more especially while I was staying at Larling, I had witnessed anything which could be presented in a divorce court as evidence of cruelty. I did my best, if only because I fancied that to be called as a witness might get me a few days' leave, but either the proceedings were dropped or what I could recall seemed useless to the lawyers.

I was intermittently aware of pacifist doings. Murry wrote in a much-shrunken *Adelphi* and was also editing *Peace News*. He was again at Langham, but living neither in The Oaks nor in Little Oaks. Murry was, in the end, so I understood, driven out by the new leader, one of the proletarian geniuses *The Adelphi* had delighted in discovering. Throughout Hitler's war, a fluctuating population of conscientious objectors farmed the land attached to The Oaks. It was finally taken over by the Home Office and turned into a reformatory 'without walls', which caused more trouble to the local population than we ever did, wreaking particular havoc in S. L. Bensusan's bird sanctuary.

My wife spent a fortnight at The Oaks in the summer of 1941, for what reason neither she nor I can now recall. To be seen, Murry had to be visited. As recounted in her book, *To Keep Faith*, he was then installed with Mary Gamble, not yet his fourth wife. I had not at that time met her. This was my wife's first meeting with her. Max Plowman died while I was in Ireland. Later, still in the Army, I was involved, on leave, in sorting out letters of his for the publisher of *Bridge into the Future*.

NINETEEN

I was invalided out of the Army in April 1945, a month before the German capitulation. In May, the lights came on in London. I had taken two rooms on a first floor in Hampstead. My daughter was then just five, my son eight months. It is one of those facts which, clearly unimportant in themselves, may yet acquire a symbolic force in the minds of those whom they most directly concern, that, whereas I had still been in my twenties when I went into the Army, I was in my thirties when I came out of it.

After some years of feeling, if anything, more or less vaguely hostile to Murry, I found that I wanted to see him again. I wrote to him, by way of re-establishing contact. In his reply, he described a recent article by me, which he had read in some paper, as 'pretty omniscient'. I found this discouraging and discontinued the attempt at reconciliation. Orwell saw Murry at about this time, calling at a flat the Murrys had at the London end of their lives, in Finchley. This is a fact I discover only from Mary Murry's book, *To Keep Faith*. When I next saw Orwell, we did not, as far as I can remember, talk about Murry.

Orwell appeared in Rosslyn Hill, one Sunday afternoon, between Easter and Whitsuntide. Under his left arm was Richard Horatio. In his right hand he carried a carpet bag, from which, first, a presentation copy of *Animal Farm* was extracted. Richard and my son crawled about the floor together and poked at each other's eyes. Out of the carpet bag, from time to time, further came a bottle of orange juice or a change of napkins. Eileen had died while

Eric was in Germany reporting for *The Observer*. She had died, he said, of pneumonia (I suppose the post-operational shock frequently called that). A nurse had not yet been found. Orwell now lived in Islington. After tea, we all trooped down to William Empson's.

Empson then lived below Belsize Park. He was still at the B.B.C. Orwell described him (wrongly, as it thereafter turned out) as having 'sunk like a stone to the bottom of the B.B.C.'. He wanted to go back to Peking, but in the meantime still worked in the Chinese section at 200 Oxford Street, presently moving to Bush House.

It was at Empson's that I next saw Dylan Thomas. An impressive number of poets had been gathered together to read their poems for the benefit of a French poet, Pierre Emmanuel. Though held in Empson's basement, this was in some sense a British Council do. Pierre Emmanuel read his own poems in French. He read well, but the most impressive sound of the evening was Dylan's noble braying of passages from work then in progress, which must have been the two poems, *Fern Hill* and *A Winter's Tale*.

In December came Michael Sayers, now an American citizen and a highly paid journalist. He was writing three separate books on England, Ireland and France. He and I lunched *à trois* with Orwell. Afterwards, Michael said that Eric was 'killing himself with hate'. In part, I think he meant simply hatred of Russia. Michael had not taken kindly to *Animal Farm*, prodigiously successful in America. But the hate he saw Orwell consumed with seemed to him to lie deeper than this. I discounted the notion. Eric had never succumbed to the glamour cast over the U.S.S.R. by the exploits of its army against the Germans at a time when those exploits were useful to ourselves. He was saying then, during the war, that the British working man's adulation of the Russians would cease as soon as the two armies met and the British soldier saw with his own eyes that the Russians were Orientals, that they had slanting eyes and high cheekbones. Yet we must not forget that the crowning horror in *Animal Farm* had been that the pigs became indistinguishable from the human farmers.

I, in my turn, now worked at the B.B.C. I was editing and producing a series of *Voyages of Discovery*. At the same lunch, the idea was broached of Orwell doing me a dramatised account of Darwin's *Beagle* expedition. This was scheduled for 29th March 1946. The mood of Orwell's script was idyllic. He had contented himself with poking gentle fun at Captain Fitzroy's fundamentalism and contriving, by proportionate emphasis, a certain prominence for the question of American slavery. A fortnight before transmission, Orwell was on his back with gastritis and wanted me to devise a concluding flourish to the programme. He did not like what I suggested. I cannot recall the form it took, but he thought it was 'casting a sop to those stinking Catholics'.

Shortly thereafter, he went to a house he had taken on the island of Jura (his first glimpse of Scotland). I was invited there for July, but in the end I did not go. Orwell returned to London in October.

The winter turned exceptionally cold. Orwell made for me a radio adaptation of *Animal Farm*. This was produced on 14th January 1947. We also discussed (but they came to nothing) an adaptation of *Boule de Suif*, an imaginary conversation between Pontius Pilate ('I have always felt he has had a raw deal') and Lenin, and a programme in which a group of parliamentary candidates should utter, instead of party speeches, their real calculations.

The B.B.C. got in the way of my relations with Orwell. In those early days of the Third Programme, I took the aesthetics of the medium with a perhaps excessive seriousness. Orwell's interest lay exclusively in what he could get away with in the matter of sexual or political outspokenness. There was no dispute. Our preoccupations were different, and at that moment I thought his attitude a bit childish, a bit old-fashioned.

The reason why I did not go to Jura was also, more remotely, connected with the B.B.C. There was staying with Orwell there at the time a man of my acquaintance, with whom I myself had always managed to get on but who was commonly regarded as of an exceptionally quarrelsome disposition and whom I had indeed myself twice seen turn on people with whom till then he had seemed friendly, once, for instance, suddenly beginning to shout at the Indian writer, Mulk Raj Anand, in a restaurant. This man had already been reported as saying about me that I had 'become very B.B.C.' (the expression 'organisation man' had not yet been coined). A fortnight before I was due to go to Jura, he had written to me making suggestions for programmes. I did not think well of the suggestions, but tried to be helpful. On his side, the correspondence had become acrimonious. I formed the (conceivably paranoiac) impression that he had decided in advance either that I was not to go to Jura or that, if I did, he would contrive to benefit himself directly by my visit.

Working for a body like the B.B.C., in which almost everyone can discover some possible advantage to himself, does that kind of thing to one's personal relations. With Dylan Thomas, the effect was different. I ought to make clear that Dylan was not, as has been said, ever on the staff of the B.B.C., but he did a good many talks and readings, and there was, in the summer of 1946, at least one unscripted discussion in which he and the Irish poet, James Stephens, both took part. My colleague, Louis MacNeice, used Dylan, moreover, as an actor in dramatic programmes. On such occasions, Dylan would appear in the Stag's Head. We talked rarely. He was generally with a group in which I did not feel happy. It was a predominantly Irish *clique* (both *clique* and *claque*, normally Louis's *claque* but always prepared to be Dylan's when he

119

was around). I could not attempt to draw him away. The occasion would have a bread-and-butter importance for him, and, presently, the party would move off snowball-wise on a pub-crawl, an activity in which I no longer delighted and which, clearly, never did him much good.

There was private talk only when, by chance, Dylan arrived early or late for an appointment and I happened to be there. At one time, the canteen in Broadcasting House served drinks. In the evening, it started serving them at five o'clock, half an hour before the pubs opened. At that time, the South African poet, Roy Campbell, worked as a producer in Talks Department. Neither of these amenities lasted. While they did, Dylan might occasionally be discovered drinking with Roy Campbell in that basement.

Roy Campbell was a man I did not know well. He was at this time a landmark in Great Portland Street. He was a huge man, with a limp and an incoherent manner of speech which suggested minor palatal defect. His face was that of a benevolent ram. He walked with a heavy stick. He wore an army greatcoat dyed navy-blue and what I presumed to be a South African army hat which remained sand-coloured. He had been the first (as he then was) 'younger' modern poet I admired. As an under-graduate, I had even, on the subject of 'classicism', quoted in my answers to examination questions his lines on certain novelists:

You praise the firm restraint with which they write.
    I'm with you there, of course:
They use the snaffle and the curb all right.
    But where's the bloody horse?

I had first been impressed by lines quoted in a review of his *Adamastor* in what must have been quite an early issue of *The New Statesman and Nation*, read in the Junior

Common Room at Leeds, lines about mountain peaks and the solitude of proud spirits. And I remembered, from his *Georgiad*, the characterization of those who formed the London literary world as

tough old suffragettes and aging nancies.

Campbell was a romantic militarist and Catholic. The first or second time we met (at a party), he described Fr D'Arcy to me as 'a good soldier'. He was inclined to hit people. He is said to have marched up to the platform and hit Stephen Spender at a lecture or poetry reading. He is said to have knocked Geoffrey Grigson's spectacles off in Upper Regent Street, in defence of Dame Edith Sitwell's fair name. He is said to have had a go at Louis MacNeice, in Yarner's teashop. At one moment he was proposing to hit me, somebody having passed on to him a comment I was supposed (wrongly) to have made. I met him at a crowded party, at which he was verbally unfriendly. Possibly ten days later, it was reported to me that Roy Campbell had, for a week, been looking for me in all the public houses of the neighbourhood, uttering threats. We met that same day, and Roy duly swung a hamlike fist at me, but in the end we bought each other drinks.

There was a lot of literary hitting at this time. Dylan, too, was reported as marching out of the Stag's Head to have a fight in Hallam Street with a man with whom he was usually on the best of terms. I understand they did fight. I cannot remember who was said to have won, though my money would have been on the other man. The horribly bloodshot eye one saw Dylan with was said to be due to him scratching the eye-ball with a rose-thorn, a very suitable misadventure for a poet. I cannot give a date to this apparition, but my faith in the chronology of John Malcolm Brinnin's *Dylan Thomas in America* is shaken by the fact that he puts the occurrence in late

1953, on, in fact, Dylan's last visit to America. This cannot have been the case, or I should never have seen the eye in that state. That precisely the same thing should happen twice is possible, though unlikely. Another possibility is that a red eye-ball in 1953 should have been accounted for by the alibi which had served on a previous occasion. My guess is that Mr Brinnin has got letters or diary entries mixed. The thing may well have happened in America. In that case, I suggest that it was in 1950. Even that is later than my chronological memory would have put it, but I do not trust my memory much for the chronology of post-war Dylan and in fact must sometimes have recourse to Brinnin's American dates.

This narrative may be conceived to have gone up only to 1947, during which year Dylan was in Florence. I had not seen Orwell since January. At the very end of the year, I had a letter from Richard Rees at the Jura address, from which it appeared that he [Rees] had gone into partnership with a man up there to farm the land attached to Orwell's house.

Eric . . . is not well and will have to go into a sanatorium for several months. But there seems a good hope that this measure will set him up again.

That was a sanatorium near Glasgow. The man up there was Bill Dunn, a young Scot who presently married Orwell's younger sister, Avril, and whom I did not meet until April of this year, when, in brilliant sunshine and over a sea like glass, he took me to Jura by motor-boat from the shores of Loch Craignish, where he now farms. With us was young Richard, rising sixteen. He also means to farm.

TWENTY

It was nine years since I had seen Murry. By post, in 1948, I solicited from him, for the B.B.C., one of a series of 'Imaginary Conversations' on the Landor pattern. He did one between Keats and Coleridge. We did not meet. I produced the programme in July. Murry was still undivorced. In August, I lectured to a conference in Oxford, intellectually dominated, as an *Adelphi* summer school had been twelve years before, by a Scottish moral philosopher, in this case Professor D. M. MacKinnon, of Aberdeen, a wonderfully impressive thinker who, with groanings and travail, visibly dragged his ideas up from between his toes. In the course of his lecture, he referred to a recent book by Murry, *The Free Society*. It seemed that Murry had abandoned pacifism. His new book demanded one last, holy war against Russia. This was to differ, said MacKinnon with a telling sarcasm, from all wars in the past 'by the apocalyptical splendour with which it should be waged'.

It was a year and a half since I had seen 'George Orwell'. At any rate, I suppose it to have been towards the end, rather than at the beginning, of 1948 when he appeared, looking not particularly ill, at a *Polemic* party in London. It was cold weather, certainly, and the translation of Jean-Paul Sartre's *Portrait of the Anti-Semite* came out that year. Orwell was reviewing, at the time, for *The Observer*. I taxed him with the exaggeratedly harsh review he had done of Sartre's book, of which I thought highly and which I should have expected Orwell to like. He said that this man Sartre must be an ass, because he said that working men were not prone to anti-Semitism, whereas he, Orwell, had talked to working men who were. He then reverted to the opening chapters of *L'Être et le Néant*, in which, said Orwell, with his thin, nervous titter, the fellow had seriously gone into the question whether other people existed or not. Well, now, this may be a silly question, but it is a question which, as Orwell evidently did not know, philosophers have gone into so frequently that it may almost be regarded as the conventional starting-point for any speculative work. At least Sartre had decided that other people do exist.

That may have been Orwell's only literary cocktail party that winter, but he was surrounded by new friends who called him 'George', and I saw him as a fashionable author hobnobbing. I, for my part, was probably in the doghouse for defending Sartre. Eric had always judged people very much by their current views. He seemed to know of only two kinds of people, 'decent sorts' and those who had recently said or written what he could not agree with. That evening, in his eyes, I must have become one of the latter. I was irritated by him, though, of course, there was no overt unfriendliness. I had no means of knowing how little time remained either for casually not bothering to see Orwell or for deliberately electing not to.

At some point in 1949, Dylan Thomas was in Prague, staying at the writers' rest home then much in the news. One gathers from Brinnin that this visit later caused him some little visa trouble with the American authorities in London. Certainly, I have one memory for about that time which indicates that Dylan remained (to me, disconcertingly) fellow-travelling. I had stayed, for some reason, late in the Stag's Head. Dylan came in, pretty sober, though it was not long before closing time. He had, he told me, just had a row in some other pub (I fancied, the George, in Great Portland Street) with a man who had been insisting 'that Russia was the enemy'. I imagine this to have been a winter evening. I cannot be certain whether it was before or after (but fancy that it was before) the occasion, in August 1949, when, in Oxford, I had to deputise for Dylan at short notice.

My old friend J. I. M. Stewart ('Michael Innes') was that year running the courses of vacation lectures, and I, with my family, was staying with him in a vast North Oxford house which belonged to Christ Church (Innes himself is a patriarchal figure, except in appearance). Dylan had been booked for a star lecture. His non-appearance in Oxford giving rise to anxiety, Innes sent a reply-paid telegram to Laugharne. The reply made a transparently flimsy excuse of the grandmother's-funeral type office-boys were formerly supposed to deceive their employers with. An aunt had died, or something. And now, suddenly, the thought occurs, can it have been Anne Jones? At any rate, I gained two guineas by filling the breach. I was billed to lecture in any case, but Dylan's place in the schedule had been more highly paid than mine. My lecture itself benefited. I was able to spend some preliminary minutes apologizing to my audience of foreign students for not being Dylan Thomas.

When Orwell was taken to hospital near Glasgow, Sir Richard Rees had set up house in Edinburgh, where (he said) the light was good for painting. I went to stay with him there from late October until late November 1949. It was in Douglas Crescent, Edinburgh, that I read *1984*. In those days, everybody had begun to take an apocalyptic view of the future, not excepting the Scots nationalists, who evidently hoped to keep themselves out of it, as Eire had kept out of Hitler's war. It seems I rather perversely said to Rees that I found *1984* cheering, since Eric was always wrong. Things Rees said about Orwell on Jura suggested a well-developed death wish. There was a horrifying story about a small boat and a whirlpool.

Orwell lay dying at University College Hospital, just

behind Mortimer Market. When I got back to London, I went to see him. He was in a private room. He apologized for the grandeur. I went to the hospital a number of times. My wife's last visit took place no more than a day or two before his death in late January 1950. Orwell had talked to me of flying to Switzerland as soon as the worst of the winter was over and the doctors would allow him to be moved. On the day of my wife's visit, he expected to go the following week.

The last *opinion* I heard Orwell express was that, whereas formerly he had always been opposed to attempts to preserve languages like Welsh and Gaelic, he now thought them worth supporting. I was surprised to hear him say this. I had perhaps been telling him about my own Welsh studies. I had perhaps said that I was going to Tenby and St David's in April and that, in August, I meant to attend the *eisteddfod*, which that year was being held at Caerphilly, within easy reach of Newport (Mon.). No doubt I also told him what I had gathered about the nationalists in Edinburgh. It was through Orwell that I first become much aware of Scottish nationalism, though to him, as to me at the time, it had seemed a mere literary dottiness. It had become more virulent since.

Dylan Thomas was all set for his first visit to America, where he arrived in February. He returned at about the time I, in late spring or early summer, saw Murry for the first time in eleven years. My wife and I were staying with friends in Suffolk. Our host drove us over to Thelnetham, where Murry had lived since the war. Mary Gamble, with whom this was my first meeting, poured out tea from a silver tea-pot, on the lawn. In the lane, a beautiful herd of Red Poll cattle went by for milking. The occasion was not without constraint.

Murry could not walk about much. He kept having to have operations on his legs, to keep thrombotic blood from reaching the heart. Betty, from Larling, periodically sent him insulting post-cards, done out in large capitals for the delectation of the postmistress and the postman. She would write, for instance:

ARE YOU STILL LIVING WITH THAT OLD WHORE?

This kind of thing did not prevent Murry from being a respected local figure. He was president of the cricket club. Garden parties and village *fêtes* were held on this lawn. It was understood in the village that even Mr Murry had his troubles.

TWENTY-ONE

The later apparitions of Dylan Thomas were so perfectly unrelated to the course of my own life that it has needed speculation, taxing of the memory and research to establish even the shakiest chronology for them. For instance, bibliographical enquiry reveals that a short prose work, *The Dead Seagull*, by George Barker, came out in 1950. So it must have been that year when Dylan appeared in the Stag's Head, just after opening time at half past five, with this newly published book under his arm. By the state of the light, it was either February or late October. I am supposing it to be February, towards the end of which month Dylan went to America for the first of his appalling lecture tours.

The first time I heard Dylan comment on Barker (who was almost exactly his own age and whose earliest poems appeared at much the same time) had been very early in our acquaintance, at the beginning, I suppose, of 1935. In response to some kind of praise of, or at least sign of interest in, Barker's work on my part, he had refused to admit anything there but 'a kind of muddy promise'. In 1950, in a satirical piece, 'How to be a Poet', written for John Davenport's short-lived periodical *Circus*, he described the typical poet of the Forties as liable to call his volume *Heliogabalus in Pentecost*, a parody, I assume, of Barker's *Eros in Dogma*. This characteristic poet of the Forties 'can mix his metaphor, bog his cliché, and soak his stolen symbols in stale ass's milk as glibly and glueily as the best of them'. On the evening I here record, Dylan proceeded to read aloud, from *The Dead Seagull*, sen-

tences and whole paragraphs which struck him as unbearably funny.

Dylan was not without this kind of malice. He collected
other poets' worst lines and made conversational play with
them. He did it, in wartime, with a poem by Stephen
Spender. I do not recall ever seeing this poem, but it was
apparently addressed to a young German airman coming
down by parachute, riddled with bullets. According to
Dylan, it contained the line:

You were a better target for the kiss.

If I could find out when the pre-war poet and Russian
scholar, George Reavey, married an American wife, that
would give me another date. It was in summer. My built-
in chronometer again guesses 1950, and, according to John
Malcolm Brinnin's careful dating from the American end,
it could have been August or September of that year. I
happened to be working at the B.B.C. on a Saturday
morning and met Dylan at midday in the Stag. With him
was an American girl, dark, with a fringe, strongly built,
not small, a bit (if I may say so without gross unchivalry)
arty in her clothes and manner, intelligent and full of
suspicion. It may have been of me that she was suspicious,
for Dylan told me afterwards that she did not like me,
whereas she did like my wife (who came in later). I am, on
the whole, less liked than my wife. This is natural and
right, but the reason given was, on this occasion, that I
was 'thin-lipped', which, in a strictly physical sense, I am
not. If anything, I am fatter-lipped than my wife, who has
one of those small mouths.

Now, Dylan was conspicuously fat-lipped. Though not
so fat-lipped as himself, the American girl was also fat-
lipped. In the afternoon, at the extremely *avant-garde*
wedding party, Dylan exhibited marked hostility towards
one of the guests, a dodecaphonal composer, who is, as it

happens, conspicuously thin-lipped. This is a simple physical fact, but to Dylan, that Saturday afternoon, it was also a meaningful, temperamental fact, and he muttered savagely about the thin-lipped so-and-so. I cannot remember by what name the American girl had been introduced to me, but I am supposing that she was the Sarah who, according to Brinnin's chronology, would be in London at that time.

There was a half-past-five encounter on 22nd May 1951, a date I am able to establish from audition reports. My last auditionee was a girl from Abertridwr, where in March I had been to adjudicate a drama festival. I had asked her to come for a drink at the end of her (alas, unfruitful) ordeal. Dylan was making his way at the same time towards the Stag's Head. He joined us. It was a beautiful evening. Dylan was charming, relaxed, sober, loudly dressed, amusingly anti-Welsh and very fat.

The date on the *Collected Poems* is 1952. It was on a summer afternoon of, presumably, either that or the previous year when, after closing time, he fished the page-proofs out of his pocket outside an afternoon-drinking club near the B.B.C. Dylan was fussed by the fact that five pages had been left blank for a Preface. He did not want to write a Preface. Why not, said I, prefatory *verses*? To fill five pages, Dylan pointed out, it would have to be a terribly long poem. Write it, said I, in short lines. Go, said I, sit down in Regent's Park and do it at once. It was evidently later, back at Laugharne, that Dylan wrote:

> This day winding down now
> At God speeded summer's end
> In the torrent salmon sun . . .

Brinnin says that this poem was finished in 1951 and that

it was begun in a letter to him. I nevertheless claim some responsibility for it.

There is on record for 15th March 1953 the performance of a work in which Dylan Thomas declaimed a poem by Edith Sitwell to orchestral noises by the dodecaphonal composer whose thin lips had so displeased Dylan. It was at midday on a Monday that Dylan came into the Stag's Head after a rehearsal. He was satirical of the proceedings and did a bleating imitation of Dame Edith reading her verse.

I had just been hugely enjoying a novel by Gwyn Thomas. I asked Dylan whether he knew Gwyn Thomas's writing and what he thought about it. He said he both knew and liked it. He went further. It was, he said, *great*. Then a self-satirical mood took him, and he adopted the pompous tones of a senior book-reviewer.

' . . . Though I am chary,' he said, 'of using words like "great" . . .'

He chuckled.

' . . . And words like "chary",' he added.

I did not see him by himself again. I saw him only with Caitlin and surrounded by a gang, drinking him off on his way to America. That would be during the week before 19th October which, on his arrival in New York, he described to American friends as 'the worst week of my entire life'. There followed the nightmare fortnight which culminated in his reception into the emergency ward of a hospital and, four days later, in his death at the age of thirty-nine.

The question is whether or not we may regard his death as suicide. That he 'drank himself to death' is certain. It is not equally certain that he did it deliberately. If he did, the moment of decision must have occurred when, between two o'clock and half past three in the morning on 5th November, he went out by himself and drank 'eighteen straight whiskies'. By the smallest measure in use, that is almost a pint. If taken in a short enough time, that amount will, I understand, automatically kill anybody, beginner or hardened drinker. I think Dylan Thomas would know that. He had spent twenty years learning about the effects of alcohol, and he was never, compulsively, a steady tipper-back of spirits, especially in solitude. Late the previous evening, he had spoken not only of wanting to die but also of his death as imminent and certain. The going out at 2.00 a.m. was itself the result of a sudden and abrupt decision. On the other hand, the evidence of the young woman who was present (and who comes over, in Brinnin's book, as a credible and creditable witness) is that, when Dylan went out, he said that he would come back in half an hour. At the end of an hour and a half, he did come back. and it was almost twenty-four hours before he went into the coma into which, if the whisky had gone down faster, I understand he would have gone instantaneously. We are not, incidentally, told whether a single barman served Dylan with all the eighteen whiskies. Perhaps nobody knows, except a barman.

My opinion, for what it is worth, is that, when he went out, Dylan Thomas did not clearly intend to kill himself, but only, in great agony of mind, to decide, once and for all, whether he would or not. I am, however, convinced that, at some point during the routine, at the second, third or fourth drink, he must have decided to 'finish it off' that way. Then, finding himself, after the eighteenth whisky, still not insensible, still able to walk, he went back to the young woman in his room, amazed at his own capacity, inclined to boast about it ('I think that's the record,' he said) and, indeed, reassured by it, for part of the misery of the past fortnight had been a fear that he would be 'an invalid', that his 'health' was totally 'gone' (and, 'Without my health I'm frightened'), in that his organs, his stomach, liver and kidneys, were too decayed to deal with alcohol normally any longer.

If that is the true sequence of events, then I think suicide must be considered the somewhat muddled, somewhat equivocal answer. I detect, in all that has been written about Dylan Thomas since Brinnin's book appeared, a tendency not to look squarely at the likelihood. This is venial. The idea of suicide is still, for many people, surrounded with an aura of primitive superstition. Moreover, though we all know that we must all die, there is also a curious tendency on the part of most of us to speak and act as though we did not know it or, at any rate, as though we thought that, barring certain preventible manifestations of human wickedness and folly (the H-bomb, for instance, capital punishment, road accident or just plain war), we should all die without discomfort, voluntarily and in our own time.

I should not here indulge in these large generalities if I did not think that at least this last was relevant not merely to what we may feel about Dylan Thomas's death but also to his personality and even to the critical appreciation of his work. Three of my four men were pacifists, Gill to the end, Murry actively for ten years. I was astonished in late 1939 to get the anti-war letter from Dylan which I have quoted. It was only in Brighton that I read, in the volume called *Quite Early One Morning*, the talk he broadcast on Wilfred Owen in the B.B.C.'s Eastern Service in 1946. I think that there is a good case (or, rather, several quite different and not entirely compatible good cases) for adopting a pacifist attitude. In Wilfred Owen's protest against war and, even more, in Dylan Thomas's reinforcement of it (for, after all, Dylan had not witnessed those particular or any comparable horrors, but worked it all out in his own mind), the fervour comes from a denial of the idea of death itself. In Owen's case I do not find anything infantile about the reaction. A young man of sheltered upbringing, Wilfred Owen was suddenly confronted with the worst that has been known in our time. In his fortieth year, Dylan Thomas was, as it seems to me, confronted *for the first time* by the notion that anything really unpleasant could happen to him, quite apart from wars or anything of that kind.

TWENTY-TWO

That was Coronation year. Dylan Thomas's death marked
the culmination of a period of twelve months which also
included Christie and Mrs Merrifield, the deaths of Stalin
and Queen Mary, the climbing of Mount Everest and
fifty-three road deaths on Christmas Eve. I do not suppose
that Dylan had much cared for his glimpse of the new
Elizabethan age. Orwell had missed it. A pity. He should
have lived to be its scourge. His last five years had been
spent in a political doldrums. From 1945 onwards, there
were, officially, no underdogs left, and everybody else
was taking up the anti-Russian line. In 1937, when I was
inclined to a pacifist view and Orwell had already seen
through the Communist game in Spain, he was writing to
me:

I still think one must fight for socialism and against Fascism,
I mean fight physically with weapons, only it is as well to discover which is which.

Ten years later, in conversation, he described the management of *The New Statesman* as 'Stalin's yes-men'. Alas,
we shall never know what he would have thought about
later matters, about the new cult of monarchy, for instance, about U and non-U or the abortive re-occupation
of Suez. Arthur Koestler is certain he would have been
anti-Suez. I am not sure. He might have taken the line
most directly opposed to that of *The New Statesman*. We
do not know.

When Dylan Thomas died, so many people felt so much

and proclaimed it in such a variety of tongues that I found myself feeling little but a distaste for the whole bandwagon. It would have disgusted Dylan, too, though, in a moment, his derision would have grown huge, fabulous and boundlessly amusing. The books on Orwell began to come out, full of wrong dates. To anarchists, he was a champion of freedom and perpetual revolt, to socialists one of themselves. The new Tory intelligentsia saw him as one in whom the Leftishness of the Thirties had been most sincerely repented, who had returned in time to the fold proper to public school men who know the world. There was even a quite specific Etonian cult. In the true, primitive sense, Orwell was Eton's voluntary scapegoat. They had loaded their sins upon him, and out he had gone into the wilderness, leaving them guiltless. In 1954, Christopher Hollis first broadcast and then printed in *The London Magazine* his story of the soap image.

Murry's book on Jonathan Swift appeared. It was praised as no book of his had been since the Twenties. There had grown up a whole generation of reviewers to whom the name of J. Middleton Murry was simply one which popped up in books on D. H. Lawrence or in published diaries and Bloomsbury reminiscences. They seemed astonished to find the book so good. The man had no obvious smell of the unfashionable Thirties about him. He wrote clearly and seemed to know his subject. Young men gave him the benefit of the doubt.

I wrote my story of Orwell's shooting stick. I gave it to *The Twentieth Century*, of which my old friend Bernard Wall had just been made editor. Malcolm Muggeridge wrote to the usual papers to say that he was about to embark on the official biography of Orwell and would be glad of letters, etc. I turned up the letters I had and began to compile a helpful document for Muggeridge. Then I decided I might as well get paid for my labour. As *The Twentieth Century* wanted a second, more judicious and all-round piece, my document could become an article for them and thus be transmitted to Muggeridge by a public route.

The first piece, 'The Shooting Stick', appeared in April 1955. It made me enemies. It was held to belong to the same category of posthumous denigration as Richard Aldington's book on T. E. Lawrence, which came out about that time. More disconcertingly still, it made me friends. Both friends and enemies thought my purpose had been hostile to Orwell. The difference was that the friends thought it 'high time'. The enemies must have made a wax (or, perhaps, a soap) image of me and stuck pins in the head, for, by the time the second piece appeared, I was in hospital, having nearly croaked with a sub-arachnoid haemorrhage, just what pins in the head of an image would give you. All this made me wonder what opinion I did in fact hold about Orwell. I had not been concerned to express a point of view. I had simply wanted to put my own little set of facts on record, for the benefit, I supposed, of posterity or, at least, of that part of it which might be expected to consist of biographers, literary historians and Ph.D students. I was no party to a cult or to a dissident faction. To me, Orwell had been a man I knew. Though I liked *Animal Farm*, I had never taken much interest in his work. I could see what qualities of masochism and courage, desperate search for experience, over-simplification and true simplicity, commonsense and foolishness, tenderness and cruelty, were tending to make him a cult figure. There was to be a legend. I might as well help to make it complete.

In September, I heard Richard Peters broadcast his account of Orwell as tutor, maker of loud bangs and nature-lover in 1929. That was a figure I recognized. This was a genuine piece, as, later, was Paul Potts's paragraph about Orwell as a maker of vintage tea. Literary journalists frequently brought Orwell's name into their writings.

Others still frequently mentioned Dylan Thomas. There was even some acerbity between the two, as between Wagnerians and Brahmsites. There was nothing in print to remind one of Eric Gill. Two of his engravings had long stood framed on my walls. I had recently had two more framed, including the under-water lady with the nice little bottom. In March 1956, Murry published his *Unprofessional Essays*. I reviewed it in *The New Statesman*, a paper Murry too had long disliked. One of the four essays was about Fielding and the idea of 'good nature'. It was, I thought, a quality that might be found in Murry. It had certainly been exhibited by Gill, Orwell and Dylan Thomas, confused as its operations might sometimes be. In April, there appeared John Malcolm Brinnin's *Dylan Thomas in America*. In periodicals, this gave rise to a great deal of cant.

In August, Murry and his fourth wife drove over to the farm in Suffolk where my wife and I were staying. Mary and he were now married. Betty had died of malignant hypertension. John and I looked at each other. I cannot have been the first to think-but-not-say that this might often have been taken as a description of Betty's state of mind, but that I had not realized it was a disease you could die of. That Monday, Frieda Lawrence's death was announced in *The Times*. Rees had not told Murry about my *envoûtement* the previous year, so that, too, came up in the conversation. Though he did not parade the fact, Murry's legs were a great trouble to him.

Yet, by and large, it was a pleasant occasion, relaxed and friendly, promising boundless future understanding.* There was no little gossip. The red-bearded sculptor was modelling my head. The *prix de Rome* architect had been reported met tramping in Canada.

That August, I was engaged in setting down my Dylan Thomas reminiscences for private circulation by the

* Murry, too, thought so, as his diary records.

American dealer with the flat in Brighton, who earlier in the year had come round buying autographs. In the autumn, Christopher Hollis's book on Orwell appeared. In November, Murry came up to London with Mary and her friend 'Val'. He was giving a talk on the wireless. Rees had us all round together. We talked about J. D. Salinger (in August, we had talked about Colin Wilson). Murry was gay and garrulous and seemed, I thought, a thoroughly happy man. A new book was in course of publication. It was about D. H. Lawrence, Albert Schweitzer, the H-bomb and Russia.

TWENTY-THREE

I got a review copy of *Love, Freedom and Society* towards
the end of February 1957. It was due out on 11th March.
I found it an oddly constructed book (no doubt Murry
would have found this an oddly constructed book). In the
main, it consisted of parallel essays on Lawrence and on
Schweitzer, first 'The Impasse', then 'The Religion', of
each. Murry had written, not only on Lawrence, but also
on Schweitzer, before. There was a concluding section,
similarly divided into two parts, 'Religion and the Free
Society' and 'Christianity and Tragedy'. This was Murry
in his prophetic role, though with greater serenity than at
one time. Over a period of a quarter-century, the wish
had been frequently expressed that Murry would stick to
literary criticism. I had sometimes echoed the wish, even
for his own sake. There was always the Murry who, as
Rees had said once, 'would be happier just annotating
Shakespeare'. And here he was again, aiming at nothing
less than to depict the state of mind in which we must face
the dual threat of atomic warfare and universal Communism, debilitated as we were by failures in respect of
what had gone before.

The 'uncouth and ungainly' world in which we live had
reached, said Murry, a state of moral 'concussion', and it
was threatened with extermination by what he beautifully
described as 'the release of the primary energy of chaos by
nuclear fission', as well as by Communist denial of that
'experimental brotherhood of love' out of which society
arose. To these trends Murry had only two things to
oppose, the frail barque of human marriage and the story

of Jesus, not as the origin of a system of beliefs but as an object of tragic contemplation. Lawrence and Schweitzer were presented as men upon whom the stresses of the machine age operated with peculiar intensity, so that it was important to the rest of us to discover in just what ways their response had been inadequate.

In *Unprofessional Essays*, the last item had been a study of T. S. Eliot's plays. Murry had taken Mr Eliot to task for the generically life-denying and specifically anti-marriage philosophy dramatically enunciated in *The Family Reunion*, *The Cocktail Party* and *The Confidential Clerk*. The new book took up this point again, more specifically with regard to *The Cocktail Party*. Mr Eliot was still represented as having stated the problem of human love in terms unacceptable to Murry and alien to those in which it had been declared by D. H. Lawrence, but, clearly, as he wrote, Murry had felt more hopeful of Mr Eliot, was merely adding in public to an old friend's advice previously given in private. For, indeed, Mr Eliot had just married a young wife and was to be touchingly seen holding hands with her in theatres and at literary parties.

What Murry did not point out was that Celia, the heroine of *The Cocktail Party*, had taken the Schweitzer way out, only ('from what we know of local practices') to have been rather smartly

crucified
Very near an ant-hill.

Dr Schweitzer had not merely escaped devouring by ants. Born ten years before Lawrence, he had already outlived him by nearly thirty. Dr Schweitzer, we are bound to suppose, was born with a very powerful constitution. Like Orwell, Lawrence had driven his weak frame mercilessly. In fact both Lawrence and Schweitzer had kept well out of the way of actual machines, whatever intellectual and emotional stresses the machine age had imposed upon them. Lawrence had indeed taken the machine as a theme for his comminations. So, with an even greater insistence, had Eric Gill. The last thing Lawrence wrote, a few days before his death, was a review of Gill's *Art Nonsense, and Other Essays*. Lawrence had found Gill's tone crass, 'maddening, like a tiresome uneducated workman arguing in a pub – *argefying* would describe it better – and banging his fist', yet thought there was more wisdom in what he said about work and leisure than 'in all Karl Marx or Whitehead or a dozen other philosophers rolled together'. He did not like Gill's Catholicism or his talk about Beauty, but found, nevertheless, that intuitively Gill worshipped the same God as himself, 'the god who enters into us and imbues us with his strength and glory and might and honour and beauty and wisdom'.

This is a god we are eager to worship. And this is the god of the craftsman who makes things well, so that the presence of the god enters into the thing made. The workman making a pair of shoes with happy absorption in skill is imbued with the god of strength and honour and beauty, undeniable. Happy, intense absorption in any work, which is to be brought as near to perfection as possible, this is a state of being with God, and the men who have not known it have missed life itself.

I had seen Murry working, happily absorbed and with real skill, mending fences, sawing up logs (once, too absorbed), laying down barrels of *Sauerkraut*, cutting up the cabbages with me on a bread-slicing machine. I had seen Orwell in this state only when he was cooking. Dylan worked trance-like at his poems, but lacked, I think, any manual dexterity. Happy absorption had been Gill's state most of his life, and, certainly, it was not the stresses of the machine age which had killed him, but (or so one supposed) fine stonedust irritating his lungs as he worked at one of his crafts, making things well.

In Orwell's life, there had been neither visual art nor music. In his writing, he never attempted the beautiful. Its place was taken by a strip-Jack-naked craving for naturalness and a certain kind of truth. His way had been most like Schweitzer's, though his effort had never been directed to the personal effecting of actual good. There is, about certain kinds of greatness, an utter opacity. Total self-dedication to a way of life which is not attractive to him lies so far outside the compass of an ordinary man that it remains incomprehensible to him and may even repel. Nobody could fail to admire Dr Schweitzer. Yet it seems probable that not many people find him an engaging figure. D. H. Lawrence is more accessible to us. His recorded behaviour must often seem painfully like our own. We know him through his bad temper, his contradictions, his frequent shooting off at a tangent, his occasional sick misery, his palpable enjoyment of places and things and personal oddities, even a certain despairing gregariousness. In my account of Orwell, just such things have been stressed, perhaps overstressed. And yet, in other ways, he was closer to Schweitzer. Short of greatness, he was yet of opaque temperament, compared with Gill, Dylan Thomas, Lawrence or even Murry. Denominationally brought up against what is agreed to be the least austere of our seven religious backgrounds, he was more puritanical, more sensually inhibited, of a more troubled 'organic sensibility', than any but the Rhineland Lutheran pastor's son. He was the most unlyrical of men, almost, I would say, strictly tone-deaf, not strictly colour-blind but without much enjoyment of colour, dull in his tactile sensations, lucky, one hopes, correspondingly in a high threshold of pain.

A Freudian would, I imagine, have characterized Orwell's emotional life as 'sado-masochistic'. True, once he became rich, Orwell aspired to better-looking girls. His *naïveté* was extraordinary. A darkly handsome young woman of my acquaintance received, on her second meeting with him at a party, his offer either to marry her or to set her up in a flat of her own. A kindly girl, she nevertheless laughed at him. The young woman with whom Orwell contracted a marriage in late 1949 was extremely good-looking, but by then he was on his death-bed. Gill was a bit of a scopophiliac, a '*voyeur*'. He was also its counterpart, something of an exhibitionist and transvestite in his extraordinary clothes. Of the two best hedonists amongst my four men (also, I would say, the two with the highest I.Q.), Dylan had died youngest. Already nine years older than Eric Gill had been when he died, Murry was still alive. I did not know it, but, while I was reading his book, a thrombosis clot reached the heart, and he was taken to hospital.

On Sunday, 10th March, the day before publication, *The Sunday Times* carried a review by Cyril Connolly, which ended:

Mr Murry's well-reasoned and passionate contribution to the problem of what we should believe ... makes us enjoy and revere his two inspired protagonists while accepting him as in his own right not unworthy of them.

Mary read this to him that Sunday evening, and, we may imagine, it gave him pleasure. On Wednesday morning, I was in a B.B.C. studio, holding auditions. Before she joined me in the studio, my secretary had had Sir Richard Rees on the telephone, wondering what I proposed to do about obituary notices. Murry had died on Monday night or early on Tuesday morning.

That evening, *The Times* rang me up at home. They had rung Rees up, too. They were uncertain about the number of Murry's wives. They got the same (true) story from Rees and from me, but the *Times* obituary stopped short at Betty, a piece of wanton cruelty to Mary, who was Murry's legal wife and had been his actual wife for fifteen years. On Thursday, *The Observer* got on to Rees, *The New Statesman* on to me. The Scottish literary editress of *The New Statesman* said, over the telephone: 'You feel as if part of the wall behind you had fallen down.' That was exactly how I felt. I took this death harder than any of the others. Odd, when I thought how little Murry had meant to me these twenty years.

TWENTY-FOUR

On Saturday, Rees drove me down to Thelnetham. With us were Richard Murry, a publisher and a bootful of daffodils. Somewhere on the way, we drank Guinness's stout and ate sandwiches.

A hearse came out of the drive, and the half-dozen cars, drawn up against the dripping hedge, fell in one by one behind it, their paintwork not at all funereal. To right of the lane, indistinctly read the top line of a notice:

THE ADELPHI HERO.

I wondered if that was the name of a prize bull. (It was in fact: THE ADELPHI HERD.) At the church gate, no bearers took the coffin upon their shoulders. It was placed on something resembling a hospital trolley.

The parson said:

'We brought nothing into this world, and it is certain we can carry nothing out. The Lord gave, and the Lord hath taken away. Blessed be the name of the Lord.'

The coffin trundled along the muddy path towards the church door. We all got out of our cars and followed. There was no choir. An elderly woman at the harmonium sang out, and the rest of us put in what notes we could find. The hymns were rather high-brow, not easy for harmonizing spontaneously. We had 'God be in my head . . .' and a psalm I did not succeed in finding and 'Jerusalem', which, eighteen years before, had been sung equally at the end of pacifist and of recruiting meetings.

The parson mounted his pulpit steps. He crossed

himself in what I supposed was an Anglo-Catholic way, then called the attention of visitors to this agreeable small church's need for funds and the presence of a box at the back. After that, he told us that he had not known Mr Murry long, but that three things about him were clear. He had been a friendly man. He had borne great suffering patiently. And he had preached a gospel of love.

All true. There had always been quarrelling in Murry's vicinity, but none of it, I fancied, sought by him. He had been friendly to me. His greatest unfriendliness had been intended friendliness to my wife. Larling would be about twelve miles north-west of here. The books I had catalogued would be sold. Murry's restlessness had once scarred me physically. A driven man usually turns out to be either greedy or frightened. Murry had been neither. There *had been* this something feverish and unwholesome. Murry's position in the new book was a deeply reconciled one, though it blinked nothing. 'Blinked'? That was one of his words, like 'burked' and 'jejune' and 'nugatory' (I had first heard from him, too, of the dreadful possibility of 'emptying out the baby with the bath-water'). The waxen peacefulness on the handsome face in that coffin on the trolley would be no mere illusion created by death's sleight of hand. He was at peace. I had never understood, and now I should never understand, *why*, for so long, John Middleton Murry had not been lazy and indifferent like the rest of us.

The parson repeated his three points, reminded us of the eschatological consolations of the Christian religion (in which his late parishioner had not believed) and hoped that we all, etc. etc. As we left the church, we should sing the *Nunc dimittis*.

I emerged from the porch as we got to the Amen. The lady at the harmonium began to play Handel's *Largo*. Among the straggle of people carefully negotiating the slippery clay between the church and the graveside, I

looked about for any literary faces. Murry was unfashionable, but there might have been a few. The tall,
brown-faced, very handsome man with white hair and a
white moustache was Henry Williamson, who, for a while,
had edited *The Adelphi* in its declining years. He had
come all the way from Devonshire. There seemed to be
nobody else. I had wondered if T. S. Eliot might come.
At this time, writers were dying off like flies. The week
before, it had been Wyndham Lewis. C. K. Ogden, Joyce
Cary (an old friend of Murry's) and Roy Campbell were
to follow in rapid succession, Campbell leaving behind
him an autobiography in which there occurs the curious
fantasy that it was he, Campbell, who shot 'George
Orwell' through the neck, during the Spanish war, with,
of all things, an orange-wood bow.

Behind Mary at the graveside, that young man and two
young women must be 'Col' (a schoolmaster in Brighton,
at work, so I had gathered, on his first novel), 'Weg'
(married to a Belgian actor and normally resident in
Brussels) and Betty's Mary (a hospital nurse), none of
whom I had seen since they were children. Battens across
the grave were pulled away. The man who had picked up
the last of them was the Tynesider who had supplanted
Murry as pacifist leader at Langham during the war.
While the coffin was lowered into the grave, he kept hold
of the batten, then threw it on to the wet grass behind him
and picked up a handful of soil.

'. . . Forasmuch as it hath pleased Almighty God of his
great mercy to take unto himself the soul of our dear
brother here departed, we therefore commit . . .'

At 'earth to earth', he crumbled the handful of soil
mechanically upon the coffin below.

I had stood at a graveside (or heard the C. of E. burial
service) only once before, a quarter of a century ago. The
man in the coffin had been my singing teacher, the church
at Marsden outside Huddersfield. Riding home late at

night on his motor-bike, he had been killed by a baker's van, swerving, it was said drunkenly, across Manchester Road. A door-handle had caught him by the neck and pulled his head off. On that occasion, the Jacobean prose had infuriated me. It was in fact over precisely this question of it having pleased Almighty God of his great mercy to take unto himself the soul of my singing teacher that my first serious, painful love and I had quarrelled irreconcilably that same evening, for she too was C. of E. and a bit religious. Later, there came the even more revolting bit where the parson says that we give Almighty God hearty thanks for that it hath pleased him to deliver our brother out of the miseries of this sinful world.

Much the same would have transpired in decent Latin if the body had lain in Gill's small, white, utterly simple and enchanting chapel, through which the liturgical seasons passed, spring never late, winter never early. The beauty of the liturgical pattern of the seasons was what I had most acutely perceived at Pigotts. For this, I should always feel some personal debt to Eric Gill. To the others, I felt no clear debt of the same kind. There had, of course, been the privilege of knowing all three, but that had been neither sought nor consciously bestowed. It was just a bit of luck.

'. . . I heard a voice from Heaven, saying unto me, "Write!" . . .'

There was that, of course.

CARDINAL

T. S. ELIOT
Peter Ackroyd

'Perceptive and assured . . . the fullest and most plausible portrait yet
achieved'
Frank Kermode, *Guardian*

'A major biography . . . the result does justice to the complexity of Eliot's
genius, and builds up a commanding case for the unity of life and work.
We are unlikely to have a better biography of Eliot for many years'
John Carey, *Sunday Times*

0 7474 0182 9   NON-FICTION   £5.99

BYRON
Frederic Raphael

'I have been reading Byron and most books about him for twenty years,
without feeling that I fully or clearly understood his life, until Frederic
Raphael's *Byron*. It is a very pleasing, quite unacademic book, fizzing with
bad taste, brilliance, and punning wit. It is the only Byron book, written
as it were by an equal, moral without moralising, sharply discriminating in
criticism and warm in affection . . . both exciting and reliable . . . without
a boring page'
Peter Levi, *Guardian*

'I found it so much more readable than other biographies of the great man
of letters and I enjoyed it immensely . . . Raphael brings out the innate
humanity of Byron and the book sparkles'
Spectator

0 7474 0205 1   NON-FICTION   £4.99

VICTORIAN VALUES
James Walvin

'It is not a book to be read by anyone who would prefer their (and Mrs Thatcher's) myths left undisturbed'
The Independent

'He deals with everything from health to prisons, from education to morality, in a style which is coolly informative yet spattered with surprises'
Standard

0 7474 0151 9   NON-FICTION   £3.99

LAND OF LOST CONTENT
The Luddite Revolt, 1812
Robert Reid

'He has written a grand book about a grand subject. Few who read it will ever again be tempted to insult the Luddites'
Paul Foot, Spectator

0 7221 7318 0   NON-FICTION   £4.99

CARDINAL

THE AMERICANS
Daniel Boorstin

In 3 volumes:
THE COLONIAL EXPERIENCE – Vol. 1
THE NATIONAL EXPERIENCE – Vol. 2
THE DEMOCRATIC EXPERIENCE
(Winner of the Pulitzer prize) – Vol. 3

'I read his book with delight and gratitude'
Saul Bellow

'Boorstin's achievement is to compel us to see again, ranged in order, the
whole mass of attitudes and mechanisms that arise from American
difference, and to display his material so abundantly and ingeniously that
we see aspects of the nation's past as if for the first time'
Marcus Cunliffe

Vol. 1   0 7474 0114 4   NON-FICTION   £5.99
Vol. 2   0 7474 0115 2   NON-FICTION   £6.99
Vol. 3   0 7474 0116 0   NON-FICTION   £7.99